Advance Praise for *The Abolition of Sex*

"Once in a decade there comes a book that breaks like dawn across a horizon of despair. *The Abolition of Sex* is that book.

We are witnessing the complete destruction of the meaning of the word 'sex' throughout the culture in general and the law in particular. The transgender movement would have us believe that sex does not exist as a material reality and should be replaced by the utterly incoherent concept of 'gender identity.' They are winning. It is the grossest of understatements to say this is concerning—it is a vicious violation of women's basic human rights to put convicted rapists in women's prisons and teenage boys in girls' locker rooms. Women are losing our legal standing and every right that we have clawed out of patriarchy, while most people have no idea. It's also chilling to watch as we are robbed of the language for our bodies and our uniquely female experiences and, ultimately, the only word that correctly names us: women.

With steely calm and acute clarity, Kara Dansky lays bare what gender ideology is doing to women—and what we might do to fight back. If you read one book this year, let it be this one. And then join Dansky on the barricades."

–Lierre Keith, founder of WoLF (Women's Liberation Front)

"I really enjoyed this book. *The Abolition of Sex* is a pellucidly clear exposition of the threat to women's rights that is posed by the politics of transgenderism. It is much needed because it is the first book to focus on what is happening in the US. Kara Dansky is to be congratulated, she is a trailblazer and I expect her book to have a considerable impact."

–Sheila Jeffreys, author, *Gender Hurts*: a feminist analysis of the politics of transgenderism (2014).

"*The Abolition of Sex* is superb, offering a concise breakdown of the legal, social and institutional abolition of human sexual dimorphism happening under the guise of a human rights movement. It is miraculously brief and readable for the immense ground it covers. For anyone not yet up to date on all the machinations happening behind the gender identity curtain, this is the book you want."

–Jennifer Bilek, founder and author, *11th Hour Blog*

"Kara Dansky's brilliant and necessary *The Abolition of Sex* brings unassailable facts, logic, and clarity to the public debate over the transgender industry's destruction of women's rights. If we as a society are able to stop this well-financed Men's Rights movement, it will be in great measure due to the relentlessly logical and fact-based work of writers like Kara Dansky."

–Derrick Jensen, author of more than 25 books, including *A Language Older Than Words* and *Bright Green Lies*

THE ABOLITION OF

SEX

HOW THE "TRANSGENDER" AGENDA HARMS WOMEN AND GIRLS

KARA DANSKY

BOMBARDIER

Published by Bombardier Books
An Imprint of Post Hill Press
ISBN: 978-1-63758-229-9
ISBN (eBook): 978-1-63758-230-5

The Aboliton of Sex:
How the "Transgender" Agenda Harms Women and Girls
© 2021 by Kara Dansky
All Rights Reserved

Cover Design by Tiffani Rudder

Post Hill Press
New York • Nashville
posthillpress.com

Published in the United States of America
1 2 3 4 5 6 7 8 9 10

*To the parents who watch in silent agony
while a vicious industry works relentlessly to
annihilate their children's bodies and lives.*

Jessica,
Keep fighting!.
Kara

Contents

Sex: the differentiation between male and female, determined by whether an X-bearing sperm or a Y-bearing sperm fertilized the X-bearing ovum, which determines the type of sexual and reproductive organs that develop, and the biological differences between females and males.

"They literally stopped recognizing every actual single woman and girl, every female person. And they told us that we were now all an identity instead of a sex, a psychology instead of physiology. That was what female now meant. So that men could say they were women. And they did, hundreds of thousands of them did. There was no single word for actual females. We weren't allowed one. Our word was re-allocated to men. We had to talk about ourselves as people with cervixes, or menstruators, and we had to agree that biology wasn't the real difference between the sexes, identity was. One by one, every reference to biological sex was replaced in every law with references to identity, until the law had erased any connection with female biology from pregnancy, childbirth, motherhood. Everything became something that applied to both men and women because it was forbidden to have real references to sex. Stating that only females were women was enough to lose your job, or even be charged with a crime. Failing to agree with a man that he was a woman was enough to be ostracized, censored, or threatened with legal action. Men took over women's sports, institutions, groups. Men represented us in every level of society, calling themselves women. There were no words to distinguish ourselves from these men. Everyone could

see the female sex were becoming unspeakable people, unspoken of. You weren't allowed to acknowledge our separate existence from male people. Men committed crimes and society said women did it. You could never escape a man because he could follow you into any public space by identifying as female. People were very, very afraid to tell the truth. Many hundreds of children lost their reproductive organs trying to become the other sex. It was a very dark time."

—Posted in 2020 by a woman in the British online forum Mumsnet under the pseudonym "Barracker"

The "Transgender" Delusion (Observations of a TERF)

I N MARCH OF 2021, a person named Rachel Levine was confirmed as the Assistant Secretary for Health at the U.S. Department of Health and Human Services. Levine is a biological male who claims to be a "transgender woman." During the confirmation hearings in February 2021, every single member of the United States Senate was expected to pretend that Levine is a woman. Every single member did so. No one was permitted to question this, and no one even tried.

Under questioning from Senator Rand Paul, Levine refused to state whether or not he approved of administering life-altering (potentially sterilizing and lethal) drugs to physically healthy teenagers. On October 19, 2021, the Department of Health and Human Services announced that Levine had been sworn in as the "first female four-star Admiral of the U.S. Public Health Service Commissioned Corps." On the same day, the *New York Times* said the same thing on Twitter. The United States government and the *New York Times* outright lied to everyone by saying that Levine is female.

On September 18, 2021, the one-year anniversary of the death of Justice Ruth Bader Ginsberg, the American Civil Liberties Union (ACLU) tweeted a quote about abortion rights from Justice Ginsberg's 1993 Supreme Court confirmation hearing, editing out all of the words that identified abortion as a right that pertains exclusively to women, i.e., female humans—the only humans who are capable of getting pregnant (full disclosure: I worked at the ACLU from 2012 to 2014). Justice Ginsberg's original statement read:

> "The decision whether or not to bear a child is central to a woman's life, to her well-being and dignity. It is a decision she must make for herself. When government controls that decision for her, she is being treated less than a fully adult human responsible for her own choices."

The version that the ACLU tweeted read:

> "The decision whether or not to bear a child is central to a [person's] life, to [their] well-being and dignity … When the government controls that decision for [people], [they are] being treated as less than a fully adult human responsible for [their] own choices."

It is difficult to imagine a graver insult to one of the most prominent women's rights advocates in the history of the United States of America and the founder of the ACLU's Women's Rights Project than to edit women completely out of one of her most famous quotes on the anniversary of her death. The ACLU's Executive Director later acknowledged that this was an error but stated that it was "not an error without a thought," and then went on to state that "there are people who are pregnant and who seek abortions who do not identify as women."

This is no doubt true, but it is also beside the point. There is no such thing as a pregnant person who is not either a woman or a girl, and there never has been. This is, of course, precisely why conservatives work so hard to keep women from having abortions.

Later the same month, *The Lancet*, arguably the most reputable medical journal in the world, tweeted an image of the cover of its next issue. The cover stated: "Our new issue is here! On the cover—'Periods on display' and the cultural movement against menstrual shame and #PeriodPoverty. Plus, @WHO air quality guidelines, low #BackPain management, community-acquired bacterial #meningitis, and more. Read." The cover of the issue stated simply: "Historically, the anatomy and physiology of bodies with vaginas have been neglected." And with that message, *The Lancet* reduced women to "bodies with vaginas."

The editor later apologized, and in his apology, added, "I want to emphasize that transgender health is an important dimension of modern health care, but one that remains neglected. Trans people regularly face stigma, discrimination, exclusion, and poor health, often experiencing difficulties accessing appropriate health care. The exhibition review from which *The Lancet* cover quote was taken is a compelling call to empower women, together with non-binary, trans, and intersex people who have experienced menstruation, and to address the myths and taboos that surround menstruation." The editor did not explain the purpose of going into depth about the health needs of so-called "trans people" (or bother to define the phrase "trans people") in this statement apologizing for referring to women as "bodies with vaginas." Why?

One may reasonably ask: If some men have vaginas and need abortions, why all this back-pedaling?

In late September 2021, the U.K. Labour Party met for its annual conference. When asked by a news reporter, "Is it transphobic to say that only women have a cervix?" Labour leader Keir Starmer said that that is something that "should not be said." Doubling down, Labour member David Lammy later said that the statement "only women have a cervix" may not be "transphobic, but it is not accurate." His reasoning was that "while it's probably the case that transwomen don't have ovaries, but a cervix, I understand, is something you can have following various procedures." One might reasonably wonder whether these men have any idea at all what a cervix is.

Notably, the statement "transwomen can have a cervix" in response to the question "is it transphobic to say that only women have a cervix" is an implicit acknowledgment that the category of people being referred to as "transwomen" are, in fact, not women at all. The category of people being referred to as "transwomen" are, in fact, men—and everyone knows it.

Thus, in September of 2021, all of this set off a firestorm in U.K. media and on social media about what a woman is. The U.S. media paid little to no attention to the controversy at all.

Awareness of this problem has been building for some time, but only recently has it begun to engender resistance. The "breakthrough" issues in terms of public opinion have involved the invasion of female spaces by men claiming to be women, particularly women's sports and other female-only spaces like public bathrooms and changing rooms.

All over the world, men are competing in women's sports on the pretext that they are "trans women," which is taken to mean some special type of women. For example, a man named Laurel Hubbard was permitted to compete in the women's weightlifting category in the 2020 Tokyo Olympics on the basis that he is a so-called "transwoman," i.e., a man who pretends to be a woman. This is said to be true because he has a so-called "female gender identity." The International Olympic Committee and the global media expected everyone to accept these assertions as true. Most people appeared to play along with the charade.

Male convicted rapists are being permitted to be housed in women's prisons with vulnerable women, many of whom have already suffered tremendous abuse at the hands of men. A man who goes by the name of Princess Zoee Marie Andromeda Love, who was convicted of raping a twelve-year-old girl, is being housed in a Washington state women's prison and has allegedly had sexual intercourse with a female inmate (which, if true, legally constitutes rape). His placement in the women's prison is in accordance with the official policy of the Washington State Department of Corrections.

In July of 2021, a man was permitted to enter the women's section of a nude spa in Los Angeles and expose himself and his erect penis to naked girls. The reason this was allowed to happen is that California law prohibits discrimination on the basis of sex in public accommodations, but it also defines sex to include "gender identity and gender expression," completely ignoring the material reality of biological sex. All of this is accomplished via the claim that men can be some form of women, i.e., "transwomen." Anyone who questions this is immediately labled "transphobic." Discussion is not permitted. This assault on women's sex-based rights is not occurring in a vacuum or by accident. It is being perpetrated by a vicious and brutal industry that operates openly and yet manages to sneak under the public radar. Its aim is to abolish sex in the law and throughout society. We are all victims of this assault, but those most harmed are women and girls, i.e., female human beings. Our society has simply not grappled with the implications of enshrining words like "transgender" and "gender identity" in law, policy, business, academia, and media. We need to start grappling with this. The time to do that is now.

The media will not speak candidly about this, and any woman (or man, for that matter) who attempts to speak the truth is immediately labeled a TERF ("Trans Exclusionary Radical Feminist"). This kind of labeling is extremely dishonest and misleading, but it has also been remarkably effective, putting feminists on the defensive as though defending our existence as female is somehow harmful.

Here is the truth we cannot speak: "gender identity" does not exist in any real, material sense, and "transgender" is simply a made-up concept that is used to justify all kinds of atrocities. It is, in effect, a *men's rights* movement intended to objectify women's bodies and erase us as a class. It is left-wing misogyny on steroids.

I say this is as a leftist and a Democrat.

Famed author J.K. Rowling recently said that we are living in one of the most misogynistic times in recent history.[1] She is right. From a feminist perspective, men as a class have always dominated women and trampled on our rights, and today is no different, except that it is worse because it is being done under the ruses of "transgenderism" and "gender identity," both of which are being enshrined in law at all levels of government and pushed by the political left. Many of us women on the political left are accustomed to having our rights trampled on by the right; we are not used to experiencing it from within our own political ranks.

I care about this issue for two reasons: First, as a feminist, I care about the rights, privacy, and safety of women and girls, and allowing men and boys to invade female-only spaces is dangerous and profoundly misogynistic. Second, as a human being, I want public policy to be grounded in material reality and science. Enshrining vague concepts like "transgender" and "gender identity" in law and policy threatens both of those interests.

I have always considered myself a feminist, although my understanding of what that means has changed over time. I became a registered Democrat in 1990. When I was in college, I took numerous women's studies courses, volunteered at the Women's Center, served on a task force to eliminate sexual assault and rape on campus, and engaged in abortion clinic defense. During law school, I volunteered at the Philadelphia chapter of NARAL, which was then known as the National Abortion and Reproductive Rights Action League. After law school, I embarked on a twenty-year career in criminal law and criminal justice, but that would eventually come to an end. In 2015 I joined the Women's Liberation Front (WoLF) and I served on its board from 2016–2020. In 2020 I got

---

1   J.K. Rowling, "J.K. Rowling Writes about Her Reasons for Speaking Out on Sex and Gender Issues," (June 10, 2020)

involved in the Women's Human Rights Campaign (WHRC) and currently serve as the President of the U.S. chapter.[2]

My involvement in WoLF and WHRC meant that I was a TERF, i.e., a feminist who cares about the rights, privacy, and safety of women and girls. That meant that I was no longer permitted to associate in so-called "progressive" circles or work in the so-called "progressive" criminal justice reform movement. Instead, I am labeled a TERF.

J.K. Rowling, Canadian journalist Meghan Murphy, and the U.K.-based Member of Parliament Rosie Duffield (a member of the left-wing Labour Party) have all been labeled TERFs for their public statements. Rowling's offense was saying that women should not be fired for saying that sex is real. Murphy referred to a man as "him." Duffield said that only women have a cervix (as noted above, the head of the Labour Party, Keir Starmer, later commented that the words "only women have a cervix" should "not be said").

In October 2021, Netflix released a Dave Chappelle comedy special called "The Closer," in which he offered support to J.K. Rowling before announcing that he is "Team TERF." He made taboo-breaking jokes about the issue and boldly mocked the pretense that a man can become a woman (or vice versa) simply by declaring it so. This set off a firestorm of debate about whether Dave Chappelle was "transphobic," including predictably angry demands from a small group of very vocal activists for Netflix to pull his (extremely popular) special offline. (So far the network has refused.) Commentator Bill Maher, a staunch defender of free speech, would later declare on television that he is "Team Dave," and called for an "honest, free discussion about this."

Many feminists have chosen to reclaim the term TERF, saying that it stands for "Tired of Explaining Real Facts," "Totally Exceptional Radical Feminist," or "Tirelessly Explaining Reality

---

2   As of January 1, 2022, the entity formerly known as the Women's Human Rights Campaign (WHRC) became Women's Declaration International (WDI). The U.S. chapter is Women's Declaration International USA (WDI USA). All references to WHRC and WHRC USA throughout this volume should be understood to refer to WDI and WDI USA. No chapter of WDI has any relationship with any entity referring to itself as WHRC.

to Fools." Nonetheless, the acronym continues to be used to smear feminists who insist on fighting for rights for women and girls. On September 8, 2021, famed gay leftist George Takei tweeted: "Quite right. TERFs are like the anti-vaxxers of the left: resistant to science and reason, convinced of their wrong position, and a real danger to others." But what is dangerous, wrong, or resistant to science and reason about saying that women have rights *as women*?

Whether or not to refer to oneself as a TERF is a difficult and personal decision. I will not label anyone a TERF because of the word's negative connotations. For myself, having been called a TERF more times than I can count, I say this: If caring about the rights, privacy, and safety of women and girls, if caring that law and policy are grounded in science and reality, makes me a TERF, then so be it.

Feminists have a saying—we can't fight sexism if we can't say what sex is. And that is precisely where we are as a society today—we can't say what sex is. We are abolishing sex and replacing it with "gender identity" or "transgenderism" throughout law and society.

Intriguingly enough, increasing numbers of lesbians, gay men, and bisexual people (LGB) are taking a stand against the inclusion of the "T" in the acronym LGBT because sexual orientation and "gender identity" have nothing to do with each other, although they are typically linked together. Sexual orientation is about sexual attraction to people of the same sex, the opposite sex, or both sexes, whereas "gender identity" is a fiction that denies the reality of sex altogether. Further, the notion that sexual orientation is some kind of identity, rather than a reality, is extremely homophobic. How can we legally protect same-sex attraction if the law denies the reality of biological sex? The conflation of sex and gender has come to be known within radical feminist and gay rights communities as "woke homophobia"—and it's coming from the political left.

Many readers will have a hard time believing the things that

I describe throughout this book. That is understandable because, on a certain level, the things that I describe are unbelievable: these include such dangerous absurdities as the mandated incarceration of male convicted murderers and rapists in women's prisons, the protection of known male sexual abusers in women's domestic violence shelters, and the complete silencing of women (and men) who speak out against these abominations.

For example, in California, it is perfectly legal for men to be housed in a women's prison because of a 2020 law that redefined sex to include "gender identity" for the purpose of deciding where to house convicted felons. Under this law, female correctional officers may be required to conduct intimate searches of male prisoners and prison staff are prohibited from referring to inmates using an "unwanted gender pronoun." This is championed as "life-saving legislation." In August 2021, WoLF reported that the main California women's prison was distributing condoms to female inmates and that one woman had become pregnant from rape. The reason that it is possible for a man to rape and thereby impregnate a woman is, of course, the material reality of biological sex, which is now being blatantly ignored throughout the California Department of Corrections and Rehabilitation. Things like this are understandably hard to believe. But they are real, and they can be documented.

This is nothing less than a war against biology, and predictably, it is creating tremendous confusion. It also presents a unique challenge for feminists because while we support nonconformity with traditional sex-based stereotypes, we strongly object to the complete obliteration of biological sex.

Often, when I discuss these matters in regular life, my statements are met with stares of incredulity. It is very difficult to get one's head around what is happening because it all sounds so astonishing. People often say things like, "I am trying to make sense of it all." My response to this understandable expression is typically, "You are trying to make sense out of something that does not make sense. You are using critical thinking and intelligence to make sense out of something that cannot be made sense of. You are not the crazy one here." So I hope that readers will bear with me as I discuss this very important matter of public concern.

Throughout this discussion, I will be focused primarily on U.S. law and society because I am most familiar with it, but it is important to note that the abolition of sex is playing out globally as well and that many of the stories I tell here come from outside the U.S. In short, the abolition of sex is not just an American problem; it is playing out all over the world.

Readers can be forgiven for not knowing much about this. No one ever reads about the abolition of sex in the media because most mainstream media outlets are actively engaged in a concerted effort to conceal it. Twitter, Facebook, and YouTube all deplatform critics of "transgenderism." Amazon has said publicly that it will not sell books that criticize it. But the abolition of sex is real—and it is dangerous.

This book is an effort to uncover and explore its origins, the reasons it is happening, and its impacts on women and girls. My aims are twofold: (1) to persuade readers that while "sex" is real, "transgender" in fact is not, and therefore has no basis for being enshrined in the law; and (2) to persuade readers that to the extent our society seems to have accepted the lie that "transgender" is real, its main victims are women and girls because the agenda is to obliterate sex. If we cannot talk about the material reality of sex, we cannot fight for the rights, privacy, and safety of women and girls as a sex class.

Many people think that the phrase "transgender people" refers to a grassroots movement to secure the rights of a marginalized community. This is not true. The truth is that there is no such thing as "transgender," which is why I always put the word in quotation marks. Instead, the entire agenda is grounded in and fueled by an industry whose aim is to abolish the material reality of biological sex. Jennifer Bilek, who founded and writes at *The 11th Hour Blog*, coined the phrase "gender identity industry" to describe this loosely affiliated conglomeration of corporations, law firms, non-profit organizations, foundations, and others that literally aim to obliterate the material reality of biological sex, legally and physically.[3] This industry is fueling the "transgender" agenda by giving out billions of dollars in funding, lobbying for the redefinition of sex to mean "gender identity" in the law, and pushing the idea that "transgender" has some coherent meaning beyond sex.

To be clear, my argument is not that anyone is trying to abolish or criminalize sexual activity between consenting adults. The title of this book refers to the abolition of sex as a noun—"either of the two major forms of individuals that occur in many species and that are distinguished respectively as female or male especially on the basis of their reproductive organs and structures," as Merriam-Webster defines it. I am also not arguing that anyone is attempting to abolish sex as a biological category in non-human animals.

Instead, the arguments put forward in this book are (a) that sex is being abolished as a *legal, social* and *physical* category of human beings; (b) that the so-called "transgender" movement (what I will call the "gender identity industry") is a key component of that effort; and (c) that this movement is detrimental to everyone, but especially to women and girls (i.e., human females).

Feminists worked hard to ensure the creation of female-only spaces such as public bathrooms, sports teams, and domestic violence shelters. Before that, suffragists secured the right of women to vote. Today, we have scholarships, business loans, and other civic institutions that are intended exclusively for women and girls—because women have historically been discriminated against on the basis of sex. The "transgender" agenda threatens all of these important historical gains and undermines feminists' ability to fight for future goals by insisting that women do not exist as a class of people.

That sex is being abolished is bitterly ironic, because feminists—i.e. those who work toward the liberation of women and

---

3   Readers can find the blog at https://www.the11thhourblog.com/, on Twitter at @11thBlog, and on Facebook at @The11thHourBlog.

girls as a class of human beings—have been expressly calling for the abolition of gender for decades. As feminist scholar Sheila Jeffreys states, "[t]ransgenderism depends for its very existence on the idea that there is an 'essence' of gender, a psychology and pattern of behavior, which is suited to persons with particular bodies and identities. This is the opposite of the feminist view, which is that the idea of gender is the foundation of the political system of male domination."[4]

For feminists, gender is purely a social construction that is loaded with various patriarchal roles, values, and expectations. For example, women in our society are expected to wear high heels in order to comply with the rules of womanhood and to attract the attention of men, even though it has been shown time and again that wearing high heels causes lower back pain, sore calves, foot pain, angle sprains, constricted blood vessels, crooked feet, and weakened ligaments. Women are expected to be sweet, docile, and subservient to men. This is all still true, notwithstanding the gains that feminists have made over the years.

The *reason* feminists have been calling for the abolition of gender is that from a feminist perspective, gender is a prison that keeps women in a position of subservience to men. For feminists, in other words, gender is the problem, not the solution. Feminist philosopher Marilyn Frye perhaps describes the situation best when she discusses the nature of this prison in terms of cages.

> "Consider a birdcage. If you look very closely at just one wire in the cage, you cannot see the other wires. If your conception of what is before you is determined by this myopic focus, you could look at that one wire, up and down the length of it, and be unable to see why a bird

4   Sheila Jeffreys, *Gender Hurts: A Feminist Analysis of the Politics of Transgenderism* (Routledge 2014), 1; *see also* Sandra Lee Bartky, "Shame and Gender," in *Femininity and Domination* (Routledge 1990), 84 ("What patterns of mood or feeling, then, tend to characterize women more than men? Here are some candidates: shame; guilt; the peculiar dialectic of shame and pride in embodiment consequent upon a narcissistic assumption of the body as spectacle; the blissful loss of self in the sense of merger with another; the pervasive apprehension consequent upon physical vulnerability, especially the fear of rape and assault.").

would not just fly around the wire any time it wanted to go somewhere. Furthermore, even if, one day at a time, you myopically inspected each wire, you still could not see why a bird would have trouble going past the wires to get anywhere. There is no physical property of any one wire, *nothing* that the closest scrutiny could discover, that will reveal how a bird could be inhibited or harmed by it except in the most accidental way. It is only when you step back, stop looking at the wires one by one, microscopically, and take a macroscopic view of the whole cage, that you can see why the bird does not go anywhere; and then you will see it in a moment. It will require no great subtlety of mental powers. It is perfectly *obvious* that the bird is surrounded by a network of systematically related barriers, no one of which would be the least hindrance to its flight, but which, by their relations to each other, are as confining as the solid walls of a dungeon."[5]

Using Frye's birdcage analogy, we can see how gender confines us. Each wire in the cage is a sex-stereotype—an expectation put on us by society as to how we should look, speak, and behave on the basis of our sex. This is what feminists have been seeking to abolish for decades. Feminists do not want women to have to conform to sex-stereotypes because they keep us in a position of subservience to men. As Jeffreys states, "'Gender,' in traditional patriarchal thinking, ascribes skirts, high heels and a love of unpaid labor to those with female biology, and comfortable clothing, enterprise and initiative to those with male biology."[6] So it is with a bitter sense of irony that feminists are now having to contend with the abolition of sex instead.

If "gender identity" means anything at all, it means confor-

---

5   Marilyn Frye, "Oppression," in *The Politics of Reality* (The Crossing Press 1983), 4-5.
6   Jeffreys, GENDER HURTS, 2.

mity with the set of sex-stereotypes that are imposed on the opposite sex—for example, the expectation that women wear high heels. For feminists, liberation entails women breaking free from the societal expectation that women wear high heels. But for gender ideologues, wearing high heels is one of the things that make a person a woman. So today, a man who wears high heels can call himself a woman on that basis. This new form of gender ideology, which grew out of so-called "queer theory" in academia, is extremely anti-feminist, anti-woman, and politically regressive.

This book is primarily about the aspect of the "transgender" agenda that involves men claiming to be women. It is not about the aspect of the "transgender" agenda that involves women claiming to be men, so-called "detransitioners" (people of either sex who go through hormonal and/or surgical "transition," and then revert back), differences of sexual development (commonly referred to as "intersex"), "transwidows" (the women whose husbands "transition" late in life and typically abandon them and their children), or the heartbreaking phenomenon of medically "transitioning" children. Those are all extremely important topics that deserve separate attention. Author Abigail Shrier tackles the agonizing problem of the medical "transitioning" of teenage girls in her 2020 book, *Irreversible Damage: The Transgender Craze Seducing Our Daughters*.[7]

The book is also not about the relatively new phenomenon of people claiming to be "non-binary." I mention "non-binary" here only because it is an aspect of this discussion that is playing out in society, and it cannot be omitted. In April 2016, actor and singer Amandla Stenberg stated that she "identifies as non-binary." Actor Sam Smith did the same in March 2019. Then came Actor Brigette Lundy-Paine in November 2019. There was a series of additional "coming out as non-binary" stories, and then Ellen/Elliot Page made the same announcement in 2020. What these celebrities appear to be saying is that they are neither male nor female. Readers who think that this does not make any sense

---

7   Abigail Shrier, *Irreversible Damage: The Transgender Craze Seducing Our Daughters* (Regnery Publishing 2020).

are correct. All human beings adopt some characteristics and personality traits that are typically considered to be either masculine or feminine. That does not change a person's sex. All human beings, like all mammals, are either female or male. Every single one of us.

The only additional thing that might helpfully be said about the phenomenon of people "identifying as non-binary" at this time is that it is inaccurate to suggest that male and female are identity categories. They are not; they are biologically based sex categories that appear in five of the seven kingdoms of life. Suggesting that female is an identity category is also insulting to feminists who have fought for decades to secure rights for women and girls. "Woman" is not a category that anyone can "identify" into or out of.

Many people, conservatives especially, like to argue that feminists are responsible for the abolition of sex by accusing us of making the claim that men and women are identical, but this is not true. Feminists have been fighting the concept of gender for decades. No feminist that I am aware of has ever said that women do not exist as a coherent biological and legal category. In fact, it is quite the opposite—feminists know exactly what the category "women" means. The ultimate aim of feminism is to liberate women and girls from the cages that imprison us. That the category "women and girls" does not exist is the central claim of the gender identity industry, not of feminists.

At this point, many readers might be thinking, "Okay, but I have a child (sister, brother, niece, nephew, cousin, friend, etc.) who is trans. What should I do about that? Just ignore his/her identity?" My answer is this: Your child, sister, brother, niece, nephew, cousin, friend, or whomever, is still either female or male biologically, even if the person has adopted a so-called "trans" identity. That is what matters. That is what is true in a material, real, objective sense. The person in question can adopt a subjective "gender identity" if she or he wants to, but that identity is no more real than it would be for you, me, or anyone else to identify as a tree or a chair.

I know that these issues are difficult to think and talk about. I know that many of us have loved ones who are caught up in the delusion—and yes, it is a delusion—that there is a coherent category of people called "trans." I have loved ones who are caught up in this cultural fad. Many people struggle with painful confusion as to whether they are "really" of the opposite sex. Many conclude that they are, in fact, the opposite sex and go on to get all kinds of surgeries and take all sorts of hormones to validate that fantasy. They then insist on having everyone else in our society act as though it is perfectly normal.

If you ask me, the best thing we can do for these people is to be kind to them by telling them the truth. We can help our children, sisters, brothers, nieces, nephews, cousins, and friends to love and accept themselves as they are—girls, boys, women, and men. Everything else is a lie. I am often told that I ought to be "be kind and compassionate" and let people "live their best lives" as they choose. Fair enough, except that I do not think that validating a person's delusion counts as kindness.

In this regard, I speak, as they say, from lived experience. When I was eighteen years old and starting college, I became anorexic. Going to college was a difficult transition for me. I went from living in a small town in southeastern Ohio to attending a highly ranked private school on the East Coast, with many people who had attended private high schools. I was very much out of my league, socially and academically. My eighteen-year-old brain decided to get matters under control by studying as hard as possible and by starving myself. I convinced myself that I was overweight, even though I was not. This strategy does not make sense to me today, as a mature adult, but it made a lot of sense to me then.

Helpfully, my parents refused to validate my delusion about my body weight. They persuaded me to get the help that I needed. They did not encourage me to take drugs or get surgery to validate my deluded ideas about my body. That would have been unkind. Instead, my parents did the kindest and most compassionate thing possible by helping me out of my delusion. That is what our society needs to do for the people who are sincerely confused about their biological sex and/or "gender identity," whatever that may mean for them.

The purpose of this book is to break down each of these topics in detail. We will examine the concept of womanhood, the abolition of sex in law, the implications of the abolition of sex for everyone, and for women and girls in particular, the difficulty of discussing these topics, and the industry that is fueling the abolition of sex. Lastly, we will discuss what can be done to stop it.

In 2014, a friend opened my eyes to the problems that the "transgender" agenda presents to women and girls in terms of rights, privacy, and safety by telling me that "transgender" is anti-feminist because it is, in her words, "the ultimate penetration of our bodies by men." Along the way, I have met numerous parents whose children, both minors and young adults, were struggling with matters of sex and gender. Many of these children appeared to believe that they were "born in the wrong body" and that they were, in fact, the opposite sex. Some simply wanted to escape their biological sex in search of something different.

Today, such a phenomenon might seem healthy and normal; it is not. The parents I have met with "trans" children are in agony. The gender identity industry is feeding their children drugs that will result in permanent sterilization and possible terminal illness. It is subjecting them to surgeries that mutilate, amputate, and destroy healthy body parts. Most of these parents are unable to speak out because they have very legitimate concerns about their relationships with their children and about their children's privacy. So they sit, and wait, and hope, while their children's lives and bodies are being destroyed. This book is for them.

Chapter 1:

What is a Woman?

O N JULY 28, 2014, journalist Michelle Goldberg published a piece in *The New Yorker* titled "What is a Woman?" The piece dealt with the growing rift between radical feminists and activists who claim that "transgender" is a meaningful concept.[8] In it, she chronicled an event from 1973, where feminists were discussing the identities of men who claimed to be "transsexuals," and where feminist Robin Morgan is reported to have stated:

> "I will not call a male "she"; thirty-two years of suffering in this androcentric society, and of surviving, have earned me the title "woman"; one walk down the street by a male transvestite, five minutes of his being hassled (which he may enjoy), and then he dares, he *dares* to think he understands our pain? No, in our mothers' names and in our own, we must not call him sister."[9]

---

[8] Michele Goldberg, "What is a Woman? The Dispute Between Radical Feminist and Transgenderism," The New Yorker (July 28, 2014). The original is here: https://www.newyorker.com/magazine/2014/08/04/woman-2. It is also available here: http://www.michellegoldberg.net/thelatest/2014/8/04/what-is-a-woman-the-dispute-between-radical-feminism-and-transgenderism. It has been archived here: https://web.archive.org/web/20210525174528/https://www.newyorker.com/magazine/2014/08/04/woman-2.

[9] Id. Goldberg does not provide a source for this statement, so it is unclear whether the statement is accurate. Another account of the statement occurs here, again with no source attributed. https://www.washingtonpost.com/news/morning-mix/wp/2017/03/13/womens-issues-are-different-from-trans-womens-issues-feminist-author-says-sparking-criticism/. "Androcentric" refers to an environment that is "dominated by or emphasizing masculine interests or a masculine point of view." Merriam Webster, "Androcentric," https://www.merriam-webster.com/dictionary/androcentric.

Feminists are still holding this line today in the face of relentless social pressure to use people's so-called preferred pronouns. Feminists do not use "preferred pronouns" (unless compelled to do so) and there are a few reasons for this. One is that we will never say that a man is a woman. Another is that we refuse to lie.

It is commonplace today to say (and to think we *have* to say) that "trans women are women." But little thought is given to what this assertion actually means. When feminists question its meaning, we are told that "trans women are women" because they say that they are. Everyone in society is expected to go along with this fiction.

Two personal experiences are perhaps instructive here. On one occasion, I was talking with a friend—a very intelligent woman with a law degree. A conversation along the following lines ensued:

> Her: Why are you so focused on the transgender issue?
>
> Me: Before answering, I would like to ask what, exactly you mean by "the transgender issue."
>
> Her: [pauses] Well, I guess I mean people who are transgender?
>
> Me: And what, exactly, do you mean by that?
>
> Her: [pauses] Well, I guess I don't really know.
>
> Me: Fair enough. Do you typically use words that you do not know the meaning of?

Her: No, I don't.

Me: I know you don't. So why are you doing
         that here?

Her: [pauses] Um, I guess I don't know the
         answer to that either.

On another occasion, I was meeting with a group of politically active women, and one of the women asked me, "What can
we do about the issue of transgender athletes in women's sports?"

Me: I have some advocacy ideas, but first, let
         me ask, "What do you mean by 'transgen-
         der athletes'?"

Her: [pauses] Well, I thought we had to use
         that terminology.

Me: Do you mean men and boys?

Her: Yes.

Me: Okay. Why don't you just say 'men and
         boys' if that's what you mean?

Her: [pauses] I didn't think that we were al-
         lowed to say that.

Our entire society needs to ask why we are doing this. Why
are we using terminology that we do not understand and with
which we do not agree? Can men be "trans women?" Can men be

any kind of women? To answer that question, we must first determine what we mean by the word "woman."

According to Merriam-Webster, a woman is an "adult female person." Oxford's definition is similar: "adult female human." These definitions seem straightforward enough. In a more
scientific sense, a female person is "an individual of the sex
which conceives and brings forth young, or (in a wider sense)
which has an ovary and produces ova." Wikipedia also states
that a woman is an adult female human, citing *Mosby's Pocket
Dictionary of Medicine, Nursing & Health Professions and Taber's
Cyclopedic Medical Dictionary.*[10]

All of this appears to most people to be plain on its face. Yet
in today's society, one can face consequences for simply pointing
it out.

In 2018, Kellie-Jay Keen-Minshull, a British woman who
sometimes uses the internet moniker "Posie Parker," had a billboard erected in Liverpool, England, that read, "Woman *noun*
adult human female." A man named Adrian Harrop complained,
calling it "dangerous" and successfully campaigned to have it removed. On a Sky News program about the incident, the following
conversation ensued:

> Reporter: What is so offensive about the dic-
>   tionary definition of women?
>
> Harrop: There is nothing inherently of-
>   fensive about the dictionary defi-
>   nition of women. That really isn't
>   what this was about at all. ...So

---

10   Merriam Webster, "Woman," https://www.merriam-webster.com/dictionary/woman. According to Merri-
        am-Webster, the word woman can also refer to a woman belonging to a particular category, such as a coun-
        cil*woman*; womankind; womanliness; a woman who is a servant or personal attendant; a wife, mistress, or
        girlfriend; or a woman who is extremely fond of something, e.g., "I am a chocolate *woman*." Obviously, some of
        these definitions are more sexist than others, but none of them obscures the material reality of biological sex.
        Oxford English Dictionary, "Woman," https://www.oxfordlearnersdictionaries.com/us/definition/english/wom-
        an. Biology Online, "Female," https://www.biologyonline.com/dictionary/female#:~:text=1.,an%20ovary%20
        and%20produces%20ova. Wikipedia, "Woman," https://en.wikipedia.org/wiki/Woman; Mosby, *Mosby's Pocket
        Dictionary of Medicine*, 1453 (Elsevier Health Sciences 2009).

that poster was put up by a campaign group that is led by Miss Keen-Minshull, who has led and spearheaded a campaign against trans people, particularly against trans women, that's extended over several months now, mostly online, but also in a real-life environment, where she sought to demonize trans women and to highlight them as dangerous sexual predators. This poster that was put up is a symbol of that campaign. It is that campaign made flesh, as it were, and for transgender people, who are living and working in Liverpool, it is a reminder to them that they are under such immense public scrutiny for every single aspect of their identity, their behavior, their body shape, their appearance. And that campaign is led by this woman, Miss Keen-Minshull, a.k.a., Posie Parker, and that's the reason why it should have been taken down.

Keen-Minshull: Well, firstly I'd like to remind Mr. Harrop that I'm married, so I'm Mrs. Keen-Minshull, and secondly, the point of this campaign was simply to highlight the absurdity that in 2018, saying woman equals adult human female is an offensive thing to say. And Mr. Harrop delightfully has proven that point by having a tantrum and contacting every CEO or every executive on the board of Primesight [the company that made the poster] until it got removed.

The reporter notes that this was not a "one-off" and that the poster was part of a larger campaign, and emphasizes Harrop's accusation that the poster was, as such, "offensive."

K-M: How is the definition of woman offensive? What a ludicrous thing to say.

AH: It really isn't about the definition itself, though, is it, Posie? It's not about that. It's about the fact that you have specifically and explicitly...

[talking over one another]

AH: You have explicitly excluded trans women from your definition of women.

[talking over one another]

K-M: Would you like to explain to us what a woman is, Mr. Harrop?

> AH: A woman is a person who identifies
> as a woman. [11]

Here, Dr. Harrop presents a definition of woman that appears nowhere in any of the definitions provided above—a woman is a person who identifies as a woman.

This notion is commonly asserted in today's society, and it is worth breaking down whether it is a plausible definition of the word "woman." First, if it is true that a woman can be any person who identifies as a woman, then solely on the basis of logic it must also be true that any person can be any type of person that the person claims to identify as. For example, if it is true that a woman can be any person who identifies as a woman, then solely on the basis of logic it must also be true that a child can be any person who identifies as a child. We know that this cannot be the case.

Even were it not for this logical fallacy, we know that it is simply not true that a man can become a woman simply by "identifying as" a woman. According to Taber's Online Medical Dictionary, a woman is an adult human female. [12] Breaking that into its component parts, adult means a "fully grown and mature organism," human means "pertinent to or characterizing human beings," and female means "an individual of the sex that produces ova or bears young." Even more specifically, a human being is a mammal, defined as "an animal of the class Mammalia, marked by having hair or fur and by having mammary glands that produce milk to nourish the newborn." [13]

So we know that the category of "women" is grounded in biological sex.

What readers may not know is that Kellie-Jay Keen-Minshull, the woman who ran the "woman means adult human female" poster discussed above, was permanently banned from Twitter in 2019. She is not the only one. Canadian journalist Meghan Murphy was also banned from Twitter in 2018 after referring to a man

---

11   Sky News, "Woman billboard was 'transphobic' and 'dangerous'" (September 26, 2018), https://www.youtube.com/watch?v=y8nViKYmEhU.
12   Taber's Online, "Woman."
13   Taber's Online, "Mammal."

named Jonathan Yaniv as "him." Yaniv had previously made Canadian national headlines after suing several beauty shops that refused to perform a bikini wax on his male genitalia. Irish comedy writer Graham Linehan was banned after he defended J.K. Rowling over comments that she had made in defense of women who stand up for our right to sex-based protections. Welsh feminist and software engineer Helen Staniland was banned from Twitter in January 2021 after repeatedly posing the question: "Do you believe that male-sexed people should have the right to undress and shower in a communal changing room with teenage girls?" This question came to be known popularly as "The Staniland Question." After appealing, Staniland was eventually reinstated to Twitter in July 2021.

What many people simply don't know, because most media outlets will not cover this topic, is that women (and some men) are routinely fired from jobs, ejected from organizations, banned from social media, and de-platformed from speaking engagements for having the temerity to say that women are female.

The cruel irony of all of this, of course, is that women have been discriminated against throughout history *precisely on the basis of sex*. In March of 1776, just over three months before the United States declared its independence from Britain, Abigail Adams wrote in a letter to her husband, future President John Adams:

> "I long to hear that you have declared an independence. And, by the way, in the new code of laws which I suppose it will be necessary for you to make, I desire you would remember the ladies and be more generous and favorable to them than your ancestors. Do not put such unlimited power into the hands of the husbands. Remember, all men would be tyrants if they could. If particular care and attention is not paid to the ladies, we are deter-

mined to foment a rebellion, and will not hold
ourselves bound by any laws in which we have
no voice or representation."[14]

John's dismissive response was both candid and revealing: "We
know better than to repeal our Masculine systems." Literally no one
is confused about what is going on here. This is about men being
explicit in their insistence on maintaining power over women.

It is no secret that at the founding of the Republic, the right
to vote was restricted to property-owning white men. In 1789, the
United States Constitution was ratified, giving individual states
the authority to determine voting rights. Not a single state at that
time granted women the right to vote. In 1869, the Wyoming ter-
ritorial legislature passed a bill granting women the right to vote
to the same extent as men. Titled simply "Female Suffrage," the
bill read as follows:

> An Act to Grant to the Women of Wyo-
> ming Territory the Right of Suffrage, and to
> Hold Office.

> Be it enacted by the Council and House
> of Representatives of the Territory of Wyoming:

> Sec. 1. That every woman of the age of
> twenty-one years, residing in this territory,
> may at every election to be holden under the
> laws thereof, cast her vote. And her rights to
> the elective franchise and to hold office shall
> be the same under the election laws of the ter-
> ritory, as those of electors.

14   The American Yawp Reader, " Abigail and John Adams Converse on Women's Rights, 1776," https://www.ameri-
canyawp.com/reader/the-american-revolution/abigail-and-john-adams-converse-on-womens-rights-1776/.

Sec. 2. This act shall take effect and be in
force from and after its passage.

Approved, December 10, 1869.

The reason this bill was necessary, of course, is that women, i.e., female people, were not permitted to vote before its enactment on the basis of their sex.

In 1971, the United States Supreme Court held that women are entitled to equal protection of the laws in a case called *Reed v. Reed*.[15] In that case, a young man with no offspring had died intestate (i.e., without a will) in the state of Idaho. Under Idaho law, the next of kin were the young man's parents, who had separated. Both parents wanted to serve as executor of the estate, but Idaho law had an explicit provision that in the event of a dispute, men were to be given a preference. So the father was made executor. The mother sued, and the Supreme Court eventually (and rightfully) determined that this was unfair.

The point, for present purposes, is that the Idaho law *explicitly discriminated against women on the basis of sex*, as have many laws all over the world for thousands of years.

It is perfectly obvious to every thinking person that women have been discriminated against historically because we are female—in other words, on the basis of sex. And yet, because the gender identity industry insists on attempting to persuade us that sex does not exist as a material reality, this conversation must be had.

At the end of the day, everyone knows what a woman is. It means exactly what Keen-Minshull's billboard said it means, and to which Dr. Harrop took such offense: an adult human female. No men are women.

---

15   *Reed v. Reed*, 404 U.S. 71 (1971).

Chapter 2

The Legal Abolition of Sex

BIOLOGICAL SEX IS BEING ABOLISHED throughout U.S. law. This is happening at the state, local and federal levels. Here we will explore the abolition of sex in law at the federal level.

The Equality Act

The so-called Equality Act was initially introduced in the U.S. Congress in 2015. I refer to it as "so-called" because if enacted, the law would eradicate the sex-based rights of women and girls. It has, as of this writing, not been enacted, though it passed in the House of Representatives in February 2021 and in the Senate Judiciary Committee in March.[16]

The bill is long and difficult to parse for lawyers and non-lawyers alike. Its stated purpose is "[t]o prohibit discrimination on the basis of sex, gender identity, and sexual orientation, and for other purposes." This is disingenuous, however, because what it would actually do is *redefine* "sex" to *include* "gender identity" throughout U.S. civil rights law. This statutory redefinition would mean that any person

---

16   H.R. 5, 117th Congress, 1st Session. https://www.congress.gov/bill/117th-congress/house-bill/5.

could claim to have been discriminated against on the basis of sex if the person believed that he or she had been discriminated against on the basis of so-called "gender identity" for virtually all purposes.

Let's take a hypothetical example of what this would mean for women and girls. U.S. civil rights law currently prohibits discrimination on the basis of sex in employment law (Title VII of the 1964 Civil Rights Act). What this means, as a practical matter, is that if a woman is not hired for a job, disciplined, demoted, terminated, or otherwise treated badly by her employer *on the basis that she is a woman*, she can sue the employer arguing unlawful sex discrimination. This legal provision was intended to remedy centuries' worth of discrimination against women in employment.

Discrimination against women on the basis of sex in the employment context is hardly uncommon. The case that eventually became the U.S. Supreme Court's decision in *Price Waterhouse v. Hopkins* is a good example.[17] In 1982, Ann Hopkins was a senior manager at Price Waterhouse, then a professional accounting firm. She was up for a promotion to partnership that year. Her candidacy for partnership was held for reconsideration the following year. In 1983, however, the partners in her office refused to repropose her for partnership and she sued the company. The Supreme Court ultimately held in her favor, in a major win for women's rights.

In making its decision, the Court noted that in 1982, there were 662 partners at the firm, and only seven of them women. It observed that Hopkins had succeeded in securing a $25 million contract with the Department of State, and that she had done so "virtually at the partner level." In fact, "[n]one of the other partnership candidates at Price Waterhouse that year had a comparable record in terms of successfully securing major contracts for the partnership."[18]

Despite her impressive performance, however, she was not re-nominated for a partnership position for one simple reason: sexism. Hopkins's (male) colleagues referred to her in evaluations

---

17   *Price Waterhouse v. Hopkins*, 490 U.S. 228 (1989).
18   *Price Waterhouse* at 234.

as: "aggressive, unduly harsh, difficult to work with and impatient with staff," and "macho." They stated that she "overcompensated for being a woman," advised her to take "a course at charm school," criticized her use of profanity as "unladylike," and maintained that she "ha[d] matured from a tough-talking somewhat masculine hard-nosed [manager] to an authoritative, formidable, but much more appealing lady [partner] candidate." She was told flatly that if she wanted to be promoted, she would need to "walk more femininely, talk more femininely, dress more femininely, wear make-up, have her hair styled, and wear jewelry."

Treatment such as this is precisely why it is so important for women to be able to complain when they are being treated poorly in the employment context *on the basis of sex because they are women*. The Equality Act would up-end this entire legal structure by redefining sex to include "gender identity."[19]

If we are going to redefine sex to include "gender identity," it would be helpful to have a generally accepted definition of what that terminology means. Unfortunately, we do not. I have never heard a single coherent definition of that phrase, despite Congress insisting on enshrining it in law.

The Equality Act defines "gender identity" to mean "the gender-related identity, appearance, mannerisms, or other gender-related characteristics of an individual, regardless of the individual's designated sex at birth."[20] If enacted, this would mean that virtually all entities, public and private, would be required to interpret the word "sex" to include these characteristics, "regardless of an individual's designated sex at birth." Put another way, virtually all entities, public and private, would be required to interpret the word "sex" in a manner that in fact ignores sex. The consequences of this could not be more dire. For example, under Title II of the 1964 Civil Rights Act, "places of public accommodation" include all of the following:

---

19   Although the Equality Act has not passed, the Supreme Court effectively brought about this same result, for employment purposes, in the *Bostock* decision, which is discussed later in this chapter.

20   H.R. 5. "The Equality Act," Sec. 9. Miscellaneous. https://www.congress.gov/bill/117th-congress/house-bill/5/text.

- Inns, hotels, motels, and other establishments that provide lodging to transient guests;

- Restaurants, cafeterias, lunchrooms, lunch counters, soda fountains, and other facilities principally engaged in selling food for consumption on the premises;

- Gas stations; and

- Movie theaters, concert halls, sports arenas, and stadiums, and *other places of exhibition or entertainment* (emphasis added).[21]

In order to be a place of public accommodation, an establishment also has to "affect commerce."

Of course, the primary intention of this law was to counter the scourge of racial discrimination, which was rampant in the years leading up to its enactment, under the system of legal race discrimination known as Jim Crow.[22] Thus, the law prohibits discrimination on the basis of race, color, religion, or national origin in such places. The Equality Act would expand this list to include "sex (including sexual orientation and gender identity)."[23] According to the language of the bill itself, this means that all places of public accommodation would have to interpret the word sex in a manner that ignores sex.

To illustrate what this means in practice, if a man entered a hotel lobby and attempted to use the public women's restroom, the hotel management would be legally prohibited from restraining him, and if they did, he could sue the hotel by arguing that

---

21   *See* 42 U.S.C. §2000a(b).
22   Jim Crow was not an actual person. The phrase comes from the 1828 song "Jump Jim Crow," which was performed by a white actor in blackface. C. Vann Woodward and William S. McFeely, "The Strange Career of Jim Crow," 7 (2001).
23   H.R. 5. "The Equality Act," Sec. 3. Public accommodations. https://www.congress.gov/bill/117th-congress/house-bill/5/text.

he has a right to enter the women's restroom on the basis of his "female gender identity." The same would be true of all restaurants, bars, gas stations, movie theaters, sports arenas, stadiums, and so on.

This is not theoretical. It has already happened. Washington D.C., where I live, already has a law like this in place. According to the Washington D.C. Office of Human Rights:

> "... if an individual, who identifies or presents themselves as a woman, wishes to use the Women's restroom, they must be permitted to do so even if the individual were to be perceived differently. Thus, under District laws, denying access to any restroom, or other gender specific facility that is consistent with a person's gender identity or expression, is unlawful."[24]

In November 2019, I entered the women's restroom of a restaurant and encountered a man. He was wearing a long flowery skirt, makeup, and pink nail polish. I spoke with the restaurant owner, whom I knew personally. The owner was aware that because of D.C.'s law on gender identity in public accommodations, he was legally prohibited from asking the man to leave the women's restroom. He and I agreed that this state of affairs is not only ridiculous but also extremely harmful to women and girls. His three young daughters were present in the restaurant at the time, and it was clear that he did not want them going into the women's restroom while the man was there.

One interesting legal question about how the Equality Act would affect places of public accommodation is what, exactly, "other places of exhibition or entertainment" means under the Civil Rights Act. Unsurprisingly, the U.S. Supreme Court inter-

---

24   District Requirements in Public Accommodations—Gender Identity and Expression—Fact Sheet (2017). https:// ohr.dc.gov/sites/default/files/dc/sites/ohr/publication/attachments/Gender%20Identity%20and%20Expression_Factsheet_04182017.pdf.

prets this phrase broadly, and rightly so. Our society has finally gotten to a place where racist segregation policies, which the Act was designed to remedy, are almost universally abhorred.

Take the case of *Daniel v. Paul*.[25] That case concerned the Lake Nixon Club, a 232-acre amusement area with swimming, boating, sun-bathing, picnicking, miniature golf, dancing facilities, and a snack bar. The owners restricted membership eligibility to white people. A class of black people sued, arguing that the club constituted a place of public accommodation under the Civil Rights Act, and that it was unlawfully discriminating against black people. Although they lost at the lower and appellate court levels, they eventually won in the Supreme Court. The Court found, for various reasons, that the club "affected commerce," and went on to examine whether the club constituted a "place of exhibition or entertainment."

In analyzing this question, the court quoted President Kennedy as saying, when submitting the Civil Rights Act to Congress, that "no action is more contrary to the spirit of our democracy and Constitution—or more rightfully resented by a Negro citizen who seeks only equal treatment—than the barring of that citizen from restaurants, hotels, theatres, *recreational areas* and other public accommodations and facilities" (emphasis added). It went on to conclude that "the statutory language 'place of entertainment' should be given full effect according to its generally accepted meaning and applied to recreational areas." That ruling from 1969 is still in effect today, which means that a "recreational" area counts as a "place of exhibition or entertainment" for all relevant purposes.

The state of California has in place a law that is similar to the Equality Act and to the D.C. law discussed above. In its law prohibiting discrimination in places of public accommodation, California defines sex as follows:

> "Sex" includes, but is not limited to, pregnancy, childbirth, or medical conditions related to pregnancy or childbirth. "Sex" also includes,

---

25   *Daniel v. Paul*, 395 U.S. 298 (1969).

but is not limited to, a person's gender. "Gender" means sex, and includes a person's gender identity and gender expression. "Gender expression" means a person's gender-related appearance and behavior whether or not stereotypically associated with the person's assigned sex at birth.[26]

In July 2021, an incident at Wi Spa in Los Angeles got national attention after a woman at the spa took a video of herself complaining to the staff about the presence of a fully naked man with an erect penis in a section of the spa that was supposed to be exclusively for women and girls. Nudity was expected in that particular section of the spa, which is precisely *why* it needed to be reserved for women and girls. The woman understandably complained about the presence of a nude man in the women's section of a spa, but the response of the staff was that because California law prohibits discrimination on the basis of "gender identity," there was nothing they could do about it. The spa was not wrong. Had they asked the man to leave, he easily could have complained in court that the spa was discriminating against him under state law on the basis of his "female gender identity." If the Equality Act had been in effect at the time, he could have plausibly lodged a federal complaint as well. Various media outlets attacked the woman who filed the video in the Wi Spa incident, calling it a hoax, until it was reported that Los Angeles officials were charging the man with several counts of indecent exposure and that he had numerous prior sex crime convictions.[27]

What all of this means is that if the Equality Act is enacted, any man will be able to gain access to any women's restroom, changing room, or locker room in all public accommodations, which includes all restaurants, bars, movie theaters, sports arenas, and recreational areas. Grown men will be able to enter areas that are intended to be restricted to women and girls all across

---

26   CA Civ. Code § 51(e)(5).
27   James Queally and Anita Chabria, "Indecent exposure charges filed against trans woman over L.A. spa incident," Los Angeles Times (September 2, 2021).

the country. When feminists complain about this, we are either ignored or told that we are exaggerating. We are not exaggerating. Allowing men to enter women's spaces on the basis of their "gender identity" is the obvious and inevitable outcome of enacting a law that interprets sex in a manner that ignores sex, as the Equality Act would do.

Congress has *already* enshrined "gender identity" into law at the federal level to a limited extent. For example, in 2013, it amended the Violence Against Women Act (VAWA) to prohibit discrimination on the basis of "gender identity" for VAWA funding recipients. Enacting the Equality Act would make matters significantly worse for women and girls all over the country.

Biden's Executive Orders

The Biden-Harris Administration has been steadily, meticulously, and viciously obliterating sex throughout federal administrative law literally since taking office on January 20, 2021. This has effectively accomplished via executive fiat what Congress has not (as of the time of writing) done legislatively. The only manner in which these administrative actions are slightly less bad for women and girls than passage of the Equality Act would be is that they are somewhat easier to undo than an actual piece of legislation, though there is no reason to hope that the current administration will undo them.

Within hours of taking the oath of office, President Biden signed an "Executive Order Preventing and Combating Discrimination on the Basis of Gender Identity or Sexual Orientation" (Executive Order 13988). The Executive Order established that it is the official policy of the Biden-Harris Administration that sex is to be defined to include "gender identity," i.e., that sex is to be interpreted by all federal agencies in a manner that ignores sex. The order directed all federal agencies to redefine sex to include "gender identity" throughout federal administrative law.

Since the promulgation of that Executive Order, several federal agencies have taken concrete action to obliterate sex. For example, on February 11, 2021, the Department of Housing and Urban Development (HUD) announced that it will interpret the Fair Housing Act in a manner that redefines sex to include gender identity for housing purposes.[28] The memo was issued to the Office of Fair Housing and Equal Protection (FHEO); the Fair Housing Assistance Program Agencies (FHAP); and the Fair Housing Initiatives Program Grantees (FHIP). It did three things, retroactively to January 20th, the day the President signed Executive Order 13988:

- Directed the FHEO to *immediately* begin accepting complaints alleging sex discrimination on the basis of "gender identity" in housing against any entity that is governed by the Fair Housing Act (which includes "nearly all housing, including private housing, public housing, and all housing that receives federal funding" according to HUD's website);

- Ordered all FHAP agencies to "explicitly prohibit discrimination because of gender identity … or … include prohibitions on sex discrimination that are interpreted and applied to include discrimination because of gender identity" (these are state and local agencies that administer fair housing laws); and

- Required all FHIP organizations to "interpret sex discrimination under the Fair Housing Act to include discrimination because of sexual orientation and gender identity." FHIP organizations are fair housing organizations and other non-profits that receive HUD funding to assist people who believe they have been victims of housing discrimination.

---

28   U.S. Department of Housing and Urban Development, "Memorandum: Implementation of Executive Order 13988 on the Enforcement of the Fair Housing Act" (February 11, 2021).

What all of this means is that there can effectively be *no* female-only housing—including domestic violence shelters, rape shelters, or college dormitories. If any housing entity covered by the Fair Housing Act (which is virtually all housing in the U.S.) wants to exclude a man and that man complains that he is being discriminated against on the basis of his "gender identity," he is likely to prevail. Because, again, each of these agencies is now required to interpret the word sex in a manner that ignores biological sex.

On May 10, 2021, the Department of Health and Human Services (HHS) announced that it will interpret and enforce Section 1557 of the Affordable Care Act (ACA) to redefine sex to include "gender identity." That means that women will not be permitted to demand female health care providers for any gynecological care in any health care facility that is governed by the ACA. In doing so, HHS blatantly distorted language of the Affordable Care Act, which does not, in fact, define sex to include "gender identity." On its website, HHS states: "Section 1557 prohibits discrimination on the basis of race, color, national origin, sex (including sexual orientation and gender identity), age, or disability in covered health programs or activities." This is patently false. Section 1557 of the ACA makes no mention of "gender identity" whatsoever.

Two days later, on May 13, 2021, the Departments of Justice and Education issued a joint notice to schools across the country to say that sex under Title IX of the Civil Rights Act—the nation's guiding light on eliminating sex discrimination in education—will be redefined to include "gender identity" for all enforcement purposes. Notably, the definition of "gender identity" put forth in this guidance is "an individual's internal sense of gender." What this means in practice is that sex has been completely abolished for Title IX purposes in favor of a person's "internal sense of gender," whatever that may mean.

And then, on July 16, 2021, precisely one week before the forty-ninth anniversary of Title IX's enactment, the Department of Education announced that Title's protections for women and girls in education, including sports, are effectively dead.[29] Now, any male student or athlete can claim to have been discriminated against on the basis of sex if he argues that he was discriminated against on the basis of his amorphous, undefined, senseless "gender identity."

All of these administrative actions are grounded in a gross misrepresentation of the U.S. Supreme Court's decision in a case called *Bostock v. Clayton County*, which will be discussed in the next section. For now, it is enough to note that the United States President is obliterating sex in federal administrative law and that his rationale for doing so is grounded in a deliberate misrepresentation of a Supreme Court case. If gender identity had any basis in reality, he would not need to do this.

Very few Americans understand that this is happening. One reason is that very few of us pay close attention to federal regulatory policy in general. Another reason, however, is that no one in the government or in the media is being honest with Americans about what these developments mean for women and girls. They have simply told us that "gender identity" is something that needs to be protected in the law, without ever telling us what it means or why it needs to be protected. What it means is the complete obliteration of sex in the law and the annihilation of the rights, privacy, and safety of women and girls. Americans deserve to be told the truth.

---

29   U.S. Department of Education, "U.S. Department of Education Confirms Title IX Protects Students from Discrimination Based on Sexual Orientation and Gender Identity" (July 16, 2021).

The Court Cases

* Bostock v. Clayton County

The decision that has come to be known as *Bostock* arose from three separate cases, after the Supreme Court joined the cases for argument and decision.[30] Gerald Bostock and Donald Zarda were both gay men who were terminated from their jobs for being gay. They both argued that their terminations constituted unlawful sex discrimination under Title VII of the Civil Rights Act. They ultimately won that argument—a significant win for gay rights in the United States.

Aimee Stephens made an entirely different argument. Stephens was a man who claimed to "identify as transgender." He worked for a funeral home, the R.G. and G.R. Harris Funeral Homes, Inc. (Harris), which had a strict dress code in place—male and female employees were required to wear a certain sex-specific uniform. One day Stephens announced that he was a woman and demanded to wear the uniform required for female employees. He also demanded to use women's restrooms and to be referred to as "Ms. Stephens" with she/her pronouns by the employer and by customers. The employer did not receive this information well and informed Stephens that the employment relationship was not going to work out. Stephens sued, arguing that his termination constituted unlawful sex discrimination under Title VII, and his case was eventually joined with the cases of Bostock and Zarda at the Supreme Court level.

The Women's Liberation Front (WoLF) filed an *amicus* brief in that case (but not in *Bostock* or *Zarda*).[31] WoLF made four main arguments: (1) "sex" does not mean "gender" or "gender identity;" (2) sex-role stereotyping, which Stephens was seeking to enshrine in the law, is unlawful; (3) sex-role stereotyping has dangerous implications

---

30   *Bostock v. Clayton Cnty.*, 590 U.S. __ (2020).
31   I served on the board of the Women's Liberation Front from 2016–2020 and participated in the drafting of each brief described in this section.

for women's employment, education, and other arenas; and (4) a rul-ing in favor of Stephens would amount to government-compelled speech, in violation of the First Amendment. WoLF was essentially asking the Supreme Court for a ruling that would protect women, *as women*, from sex discrimination in the employment arena.

Stephens ultimately won before the Supreme Court, which ruled that discrimination on the basis of "transgender status" constitutes unlawful sex discrimination in the employment con-text. Unhelpfully, the Court did not provide a definition of what "transgender status" might mean. Instead, it appeared to simply assume that everybody knows what it means. In any event, what-ever "transgender status" means, the United States Supreme Court has now officially used it to erase sex in its enforcement of the legal prohibition on sex discrimination in employment.

As explained above, the Biden administration is grossly mis-representing the ruling in *Bostock* to justify the abolition of sex throughout federal administrative law. Whatever one might say about *Bostock*, the Court expressly limited its ruling to the Title VII (employment) context. The court stated explicitly:

> "The employers worry that our decision will sweep beyond Title VII to other feder-al and state laws that prohibit sex discrim-ination. And, under Title VII itself, they say sex-segregated bathrooms, locker rooms, and dress codes will prove unsustainable after our decision today. But none of these other laws are before us; we have not had the benefit of adversarial testing about the meaning of their terms, and we do not prejudge any such ques-tion today. Under Title VII, too, we do not purport to address bathrooms, locker rooms, or anything else of the kind. The only ques-

> tion before us is whether an employer who
> fires someone simply for being homosexual or
> transgender has discharged or otherwise dis-
> criminated against that individual "because of
> such individual's sex."

Despite this express limitation by the Supreme Court in the scope of its own ruling, all of the Biden administration's executive orders mandating the abolition of sex in federal administrative law—in healthcare, housing, education, and so forth—state that they are based on the *Bostock* ruling.

There is a second way in which the administration is misconstruing *Bostock*. The Court stated that Stephens was protected on the basis of his "transgender status" (again, without ever once defining "transgender status"). But the executive orders state that *Bostock* requires the protection of "gender identity" as sex. As bad as the *Bostock* decision is for women and girls, it cannot accurately be said that the Court required that sex be defined to include "gender identity." In fact, it expressly declined to rule on that question:

> "Appealing to roughly contemporaneous
> dictionaries, the employers say that, as used
> here, the term "sex" in 1964 referred to "sta-
> tus as either male or female [as] determined by
> reproductive biology." The employees count-
> er by submitting that, even in 1964, the term
> bore a broader scope, capturing more than
> anatomy and reaching at least some norms
> concerning gender identity and sexual orienta-
> tion. But because nothing in our approach to
> these cases turns on the outcome of the parties'
> debate, and because the employees concede the
> point for argument's sake, we proceed on the

assumption that "sex" signified what the employers suggest, referring only to biological distinctions between male and female."

The Biden administration is simply lying about the outcome of the *Bostock* case, and we must ask ourselves why.

The *Bostock* ruling did not appear in a vacuum. Several cases about "gender identity" have been bouncing around in the federal judiciary for several years. Here I will address a few of them.

* Gloucester County School Board v. Grimm

The Gavin Grimm case has had a long and somewhat tortured six-year history, with many twists and turns. My summary will undoubtedly omit certain details; my hope is simply to provide an overview of this very strange case because it provides a glimpse into the abolition of sex in the law.

The case began in 2015, when Gavin legally challenged a newly adopted policy of the Gloucester County school board, where Gavin was attending high school. Gavin is biologically female but claims to "identify as male." The policy that Gavin was challenging required students to use *either* multi-user restrooms that correspond with their biological sex *or* newly constructed single-user restrooms available to either sex. Gavin was unsatisfied with this entirely reasonable policy, however, because she wanted to be able to use the boys' facilities. So, Gavin sued the school board, arguing that the policy violated both Title IX and the Equal Protection Clause of the 14th Amendment. Gavin's complaint was dismissed, however, because of a federal regulation that expressly allows Title IX funding recipients (including Gavin's school) to maintain separate facilities, including bathrooms, *on the basis of sex*.

Gavin appealed, and the appellate court (the U.S. Court of Appeals for the Fourth Circuit) reversed the dismissal. In doing so, the appellate court ruled that the regulation in question was "ambiguous" about "whether a transgender individual is a male or female for the purpose of access to sex-segregated restrooms." This is an astonishing statement to be issued by a United States federal court. The regulation in question was promulgated in 1975 as a mechanism for enforcing Title IX. It essentially says that although Title IX prohibits sex discrimination in the educational arena, funding recipients are permitted to maintain sex-specific restrooms, locker rooms, and the like. This is an entirely reasonable, common-sense approach to dealing with sex discrimination in education.

However, in 2016, the Obama Administration had issued a letter to schools, instructing Title IX recipients to interpret the word sex to include "gender identity," and the Fourth Circuit found that letter to be a sufficient basis on which to ignore the regulation. Essentially, the court, consisting of federal judges who enjoy lifetime appointments, found that the regulation protecting single-sex spaces is ambiguous. WoLF filed an *amicus* brief, arguing (among other things) that redefining sex to mean "gender identity" would be terrible public policy because of women's privacy and safety concerns, pointing out the importance of addressing historical and systemic discrimination against women and girls, and noting the fact that "gender identity" erases women. But the court ignored WoLF's concerns. If this all sounds bizarre to readers, that's because it is.

The school board sought review in the Supreme Court, and the Court accepted. This time, WoLF filed two *amicus* briefs—one in favor of the Court taking up the case and another in favor of a ruling confirming that, in fact, sex matters. However, in the meantime the administration had changed hands and had withdrawn the letter that the Obama administration previously issued. The Supreme Court then sent the case back to the Fourth Circuit, which in turn sent it back to the original court. That court (which had dismissed Gavin's original complaint) ruled in Gavin's favor.

This time, on appeal, the Fourth Circuit again simply ignored the material reality of biological sex and affirmed the favorable ruling. In doing so, it extended the reasoning of the *Bostock* decision to the Title IX context and stated that the Board's policy of maintaining sex-specific facilities meant it was "rely[ing] on its own discriminatory notions of what 'sex' means." Thus, according to the U.S. Court of Appeals for the Fourth Circuit, acknowledging the material reality of sex is, itself, discriminatory.

On June 28, 2021, the Supreme Court announced that it would not review that decision, so the Fourth Circuit's decision stands, and the matter is final. What this means in practice is that throughout the Fourth Circuit (which encompasses the states of Maryland, Virginia, West Virginia, North Carolina, and South Carolina), there is effectively no such thing as single-sex facilities in federally funded schools.

* Doe v. Boyertown Area School District

At the beginning of the 2016–2017 school year, Joel Doe was a student in the Boyertown Area School District, outside of Philadelphia.[32] That year, the district had adopted a new policy of allowing students to use restrooms and locker rooms that corresponded to their "gender identity," rather than their sex, following the letter issued by the Obama Administration. The district did this with no notice to students or parents.

Joel first learned about this new policy when he was changing in the boys' locker room, wearing only his underwear, and looked up to see a female student nearby. He was extremely uncomfortable about this and complained to school administrators, but he was ignored. Joel wasn't alone. It turned out that there were several students who were extremely unhappy about this policy—both girls and boys. Several of these students simply stopped using the facilities. Joel Doe was later punished for refusing to change clothes for gym class because he was not comfortable using the boys' locker room when girls were present.

---

32   All of the students involved in this matter are listed pseudonymously in court documents. One of the plaintiffs, Mary Smith, decided to use her real name, Alexis Lightcap, after she graduated from high school. In May 2018, Alexis published a piece in the Philadelphia Inquirer about her ordeal. *See* Alexis Lightcap, "Girls and Boys Shouldn't Do Everything Together," Philadelphia Inquirer (May 24, 2018).

The students sued the district in federal court and lost. They appealed to the U.S. Court of Appeals for the Third Circuit and lost again. During oral arguments before the Circuit's three-judge panel, one judge admonished the attorney for the students not to use the phrase "opposite sex" during arguments because he found that the phrase "complicates the discussion."[33] But it is utterly unclear why a federal judge would find this phrase "complicated." The Supreme Court used the phrase "opposite sex" four times in its decision in *Obergefell v. Hodges*, the landmark decision ruling that states cannot prohibit same-sex marriage, seemingly without any confusion or complication.[34]

The Third Circuit's reasoning for its decision was that the district's policy of allowing students to use the facilities that corresponded with their "gender identity" regardless of sex "served a compelling interest—preventing discrimination against transgender students—and was narrowly tailored to that interest." Never mind the district's compelling interest in protecting students' privacy from the opposite sex. To justify its decision, the court appears to have decided that a male student who claims to "identify as female" is, in fact, female, and vice versa. The court went on to criticize the students—teenagers—for refusing to embrace the idea that their right not to be among members of the opposite sex depends on what someone else believes about "gender identity."

The students sought review in the Supreme Court, asking the Court to address these questions:

- Given students' constitutionally protected privacy interest in their partially clothed bodies, whether a public school has a compelling interest in authorizing students who believe themselves to be members of the opposite sex to use locker rooms and restrooms reserved exclusively for the opposite sex, and whether such a policy is narrowly tailored.

---

33   Oral Argument at 4:22, Boyertown (No. 17-3113), https://www2.ca3.uscourts.gov/oralargument/audio/17-3113Doev.BoyertownAreaSchoolDist.mp3.
34   *See, e.g., Obergefell v. Hodges* 135 S. Ct. 2584, 2593 (2015) ("The petitioners in these cases seek to find that liberty by marrying someone of the same sex and having their marriages deemed lawful on the same terms and conditions as marriages between persons of the opposite sex.").

- Whether the Boyertown policy constructively denies access to locker room and restroom facilities under Title IX "on the basis of sex."

Those questions sound like they might be legally complicated, but they really are not. The first employs language that courts typically use when discussing equal protection of the law under the 14th Amendment. The second is essentially a question about whether schools may maintain sex-specific facilities under Title IX. Another way of asking these questions is, basically, "can schools legally, i.e., consistent with applicable statutory and constitutional law, acknowledge the material reality of sex?"

WoLF filed another *amicus* brief urging the Court to take up the case. Its appeal presented five arguments for the Court's consideration: (1) if "gender identity" is used to interpret the constitutional right to privacy and Title IX, women and girls will lose their privacy and be put at even greater risk; (2) if "gender identity" is used to interpret Title IX, women and girls will lose preferences addressing historical and systemic discrimination; (3) women and girls will lose preferences under other remedial statutes; (4) civil rights protections should not be based on subjective feelings; and (5) replacing sex with "gender identity" under civil rights law will distort vital statistics.

The Supreme Court declined to hear the case.

It is extremely unfortunate that the Court did not take up this case, and that it *did* take up the case of Aimee Stephens. Both cases presented opportunities to examine important questions of sex and gender, but the *Boyertown* case would have been a much more straightforward avenue for doing it. *Boyertown* presented extremely clean questions, whereas *Stephens* presented much more complicated questions about the extent to which the case was about dress codes (it was not), the appropriateness of examining questions about sexual orientation and "gender identity" in conjunction with one another, and the applicability of prohibitions on sex-stereotyping. None of those complicated questions was before the Court in *Boyertown*.

The Supreme Court has absolute discretion on which cases to take up. There is no rule requiring it to announce its reasons for doing or not doing so, and it rarely does announce its rationale, so there is never any way to know for certain. But if one were to speculate, one might wonder whether it did not take up *Boyertown* precisely *because* it did not want to answer the very straightforward question of whether schools can legally, consistent with applicable statutory and constitutional law, acknowledge the material reality of sex. Regardless, the Court has clearly contributed to the abolition of sex in the law.

As with *Gloucester County*, the Court's decision not to take up the case puts an end to the matter. So, for now, throughout the Third Circuit (which encompasses Pennsylvania, New Jersey, Delaware, and the Virgin Islands), as in the Fourth, single-sex facilities in publicly funded schools are a thing of the past.

* Soule v. Connecticut Association of Schools

Selina Soule, Chelsea Mitchell, Alanna Smith, and Ashley Nicoletti are all female track athletes. In 2020, Selina and Chelsea were seniors and Alanna and Ashley were sophomores in Connecticut high schools. Selina and Chelsea have since graduated. All of them train hard to win events, boost confidence, and gain opportunities to compete for medals, college admissions, and scholarships.

The Connecticut Interscholastic Athletic Conference is the sole governing body for inter-scholastic athletic activities in Connecticut and directs and controls high school athletics for boys and girls in the state. At some point, the CIAC adopted a policy of deferring to the "determination of the student and his or her local school regarding gender identification" and now requires a school district to "determine a student's eligibility to participate in a CIAC gender-specific sports team based on the gender identification of that student in current school records and daily life activities in the school and community ..."[35] On the basis of this

---

35   Connecticut Interscholastic Association of Schools, "Reference Guide for Transgender Policy," Article IX, Section B. https://www.casciac.org/pdfs/Principal_Transgender_Discussion_Quick_Reference_Guide.pdf.

policy, all four of the girls at some point, in order to compete in girls' track, had to compete against two boys after the boys and their schools asserted that they had a female "gender identity." The girls lost events and opportunities to these two male athletes who claim to "identify as female" as a result of this policy, so they sued the CIAC (among others) in federal court.

The problems with the CIAC policy are immediately obvious to everyone who understands that sex is grounded in material reality, but to put it in the girls' words (from the initial Complaint):

> "Unfortunately for Plaintiffs and other girls in Connecticut, those dreams and goals—those opportunities for participation, recruitment, and scholarships—are now being directly and negatively impacted by a new policy that is permitting boys who are male in every biological respect to compete in girls' athletic competitions if they claim a female gender identity.

> This discriminatory policy is now regularly resulting in boys displacing girls in competitive track events in Connecticut—excluding specific and identifiable girls including Plaintiffs from honors, opportunities to compete at higher levels, and public recognition critical to college recruiting and scholarship opportunities that should go to those outstanding female athletes."

Shortly after the Complaint was filed in February 2020, the two boys moved to intervene as defendants. They eventually won that motion. But in the meantime, an interesting series of events occurred during the course of the litigation that reveal a lot about the abolition of sex in the federal judiciary.

During a hearing on the boys' motion to intervene, the court ordered the girls' attorney not to refer to intervenors as "males" but instead as "transgender females." The judge later acknowledged that the attorney was not prohibited from mentioning the fact that the boys had male bodies but maintained his prohibition on the use of the word "male" to describe them.

As any thinking person can see, this makes absolutely no sense whatsoever. The attorney subsequently filed a motion for the judge to disqualify himself on the basis that he was exhibiting clear bias against the girls. In doing so, the attorney argued that the judge's order "created rather than avoided [an] appearance of bias on matters at this lawsuit's heart: whether by allowing males to take victories and opportunities away from females in separate athletic competitions designated for girls, the challenged policy deprives the Plaintiffs of rights guaranteed to them by Title IX."

Crucially, for present purposes, the motion stated that "references to individuals as 'transgender females' obscures and rejects the binary of reproductive biology and declares that there is a third (at least) category relevant to [the girls'] claims. More, it is a declaration that, as between subjective gender identity (female) and objective reproductive biology (male), the subjective is the more important and essential 'truth.'"

And here we arrive at the crux of the matter: at least one sitting judge with a lifetime appointment on the United States judiciary has capitulated not only to the idea that males can be female but also to the idea that subjective belief is more important than objective, scientific truth when deciding matters of law.

Unsurprisingly, the judge denied the motion that he recuse himself in a cursory order that contained no citation or discussion of relevant legal precedent or standards. The attorney appealed to the 2nd Circuit in a 289-page writ of mandamus that contained a detailed explanation as to why the writ was necessary, including voluminous discussion of the relevant precedents and an addendum containing all the pertinent documents. The 2nd Circuit summarily denied the writ without comment.

So, the matter proceeded (at a snail's pace) before the original court, which eventually dismissed the girls' complaint on the basis that the matter had become moot because the male athletes had graduated from high school. The girls appealed, and at this time, the matter is pending before the 2nd Circuit Court of Appeals.

We will, at some point, learn whether the 2nd Circuit will join the 3rd and 4th in abolishing sex and obliterating sex-specific spaces and sports teams.

* Hecox v. Little

On March 30, 2020, Idaho Governor Bradley Little signed the Fairness in Women's Sports Act. It became the first law in the United States to keep women's sports limited to women. Between 2020 and 2021, over thirty-seven states would enact or consider similar types of legislation. In December 2020, shortly before leaving office, former Democratic House Representative Tulsi Gabbard introduced the Protect Women's Sports Act in the House of Representatives, but because she had already declined to run to keep her seat, the bill died before advancing. Beth Stelzer tracks the progress of all of this legislation on her website Save Women's Sports.[36]

On April 15, 2020, a young man named Lindsay Hecox, represented by the ACLU, filed suit in federal court to challenge the Idaho law. Lindsay argued that the law violated his constitutional rights to equal protection, due process, informational privacy, and freedom from unlawful search and seizure, and also that it violated Title IX because he "is an adult woman" and that he "is transgender." His basic argument is that he, an "adult woman" who "is transgender" has a legal and constitutional right to compete in women's sports and that because state law limited women's sports to women, i.e., female people, his rights are being violated.

It is worth taking a moment to note the use of language here. The ACLU is telling a federal court that Lindsay, a male person, is an "adult woman." Later in the complaint, the ACLU states that

36   Save Women's Sports, https://savewomenssports.com/ (2021).

"[g]ender identity is the medical term for a person's internal, innate sense of belonging to a particular sex." But it is simply not the case that a person's sex is based on an internal, innate sense of anything. This simply is a gross misrepresentation of reality. Lindsay's complaint continues: "The term 'biological sex' is imprecise. A person's sex encompasses several different biological attributes, including certain chromosomes, certain genes, gonads, the body's production of and response to certain hormones, internal and external genitalia, secondary sex characteristics, and gender identity. Those attributes are not always aligned in typical ways." It is, of course, true that some people have what are often referred to as "intersex" conditions, or "differences of sexual development," which occur when a person's chromosomal make-up varies from either XX or XY (a phenomenon that occurs in approximately .02 percent of the population). But that is a far cry from sex being an "internal, innate sense."

In any event, Lindsay and the ACLU succeeded in persuading the court to abolish sex when, in August 2020, the court granted Lindsay's motion for a preliminary injunction, which meant that the law was stopped from going into effect. In the meantime, two female athletes, Madison Kenyon and Mary Marshall, intervened in the case to join the state as defendants. The state and the intervenors appealed, and the case went before the 9th Circuit Court of Appeals. Rather than rule on the merits of the case, however, the 9th Circuit determined that there remained factual questions about whether the case had become moot (for example, Lindsay had since dropped out of college), and sent the case back to the lower court to answer those questions. At the time of writing, the case is before the lower court to answer those questions.

If Lindsay eventually prevails before the U.S. Court of Appeals for the 9th Circuit, it will mean that throughout the Circuit (which encompasses the states of Alaska, Arizona, California, Hawaii, Idaho, Montana, Nevada, Oregon, and Washington), there will be no such thing as sex-specific spaces or sports in schools, unless the state asks the Supreme Court to review the matter and the Supreme Court reverses.

* B.J.P. v. West Virginia State Board of Education

The problem of U.S. federal courts abolishing sex is getting even worse. B.J.P. (as identified in pertinent court documents) is a biologically male student who wishes to participate in girls' cross country and track in West Virginia.[37] Because the state recently passed a law limiting participation in girls' athletics to actual girls, B.J.P.'s school said no, and B.J.P. sued. In July 2021, the U.S. District Court for the Southern District of West Virginia blocked the law, ruling that B.J.P. was likely to eventually prove that it is unconstitutional.

In doing so, it accepted at face value that B.J.P. is actually a girl (noting that B.J.P. went on puberty-blocking hormones at the age of nine) and found that B.J.P. would have no competitive advantage over girls. The court also cited the Fourth Circuit's opinion in *Grimm* for the proposition that "transgender" is "used as an umbrella term to describe groups of people who transcend conventional expectations of gender identity or expression."

But this is silly. Even assuming that B.J.P. does, in fact, "transcend conventional expectations," the only way that that fact magically turns B.J.P. into a girl is if the material reality of sex is irrelevant. It ought to be fine for kids to look and behave in ways that defy society's expectations of what girls and boys are supposed to do without suggesting that such defiance turns kids into the opposite sex.

Again and again, students and state governments are asking the federal judiciary to confirm that sex matters and that women and girls have the right to spaces and sports, separate from men and boys. Again and again, the courts have disappointed them by abolishing sex as a meaningful category in the law.

Abolishing sex as a meaningful category in the law has grave implications for everyone, but especially for women and girls, which will be explored in the next chapter.

---

37   *B.J.P. v. West Virginia State Board of Education*, 2:21-cv-00316 (S.D. WV July 21, 2021).

Chapter 3

Implications for Women and Girls of Abolishing Sex

DESPITE ALL OF THIS, our nation has not grappled with the long-term impacts of abolishing sex, and it is not at all clear whether lawmakers, executive officials, or judges have thought any of this through.

For example, what will come of the reporting on crime and the recording of crime statistics as we continue to abolish sex? It has become commonplace for reporters to report on horrific crimes as being committed by women when they were in fact committed by men. One of the most egregious examples is the reporting on the case of Jakob Nieves, who was convicted in August 2020 of two counts of sexual exploitation of children, one count of distribution of child pornography, and one count of possession of child pornography. Jakob is a man who also claims to "identify" as a woman. Reports of the story frequently contain headlines such as this one from the *Eagle-Tribune* in North Andover, Massachusetts: "Woman gets 30 years for child sex abuse."[38]

The article clarifies that Nieves "identifies and lives as a female" (without explaining what that might mean when referring to a man) and uses "she" and "her" in describing him. Two of Nieves's victims were under four years old, and Nieves apparent-

---

38   Jill Harmacinski, "Woman gets 30 years for child sex abuse," Eagle-Tribune (June 10, 2021).

ly told an undercover officer that "she had sexually abused two children known to her, and sent the undercover agent images and videos that Nieves had produced, which depicted Nieves sexually abusing one of those children." This is a *male* child sexual abuser being reported on *as though he were a woman* in what is presumably an otherwise reputable publication. However, no reader would know that by simply reading the headline. Any average reader would simply assume that these horrible crimes had been committed by a woman.

Another example is John Collins of Miami, Florida who, at the time of writing, is facing multiple robbery charges in connection with a scheme of allegedly providing wealthy men with alcohol and/or drugs and then stealing their property. One headline reads: "Prosecutors: Woman accused of drugging men, stealing high-end watches across South Florida."[39]Another reads: "Woman Arrested After String of Watch Robberies: Police."[40]

Any average reader coming across these headlines would reasonably assume that these crimes had, in fact, been committed by a woman. Only by reading the first story itself does a reader come across this statement: "When the prosecutor asked in court how Collins would like to be addressed, the 29-year-old said she identifies as a woman." The prosecutor then went on to refer to Collins using "she" throughout the remainder of the proceeding.

In both of these instances, although the reporters egregiously used headlines which suggest that the perpetrators are women, they at least managed to report the fact that these are not actual women, in some fashion. Sometimes, however, reporters fail to note that fact at all. Take, for example, Victoria Midrange (this case is from Wales, but the principle is the same). Midrange was convicted of burglary in December 2020, having previously been convicted of eighty-two offenses, including robbery, causing dangerous death by dangerous driving, house burglaries, and more

---

39   Sheldon Fox, "Prosecutors: Woman accused of drugging men, stealing high-end watches across South Florida," 7 News Miami (June 10, 2021).

40   Brickell, "Woman Arrested After Series of Expensive Watch Robberies: Police," NBC6 (June 11, 2021).

than forty non-dwelling burglaries, one of which involved a burglary of a police station. One headline reads: "Woman puts on hi-vis jacket to burgle key workers' hotel in Swansea."[41]

The reporter uses "she" and "her" throughout, and *at no point does the article so much as mention that this suspect is biologically male.* The only hint that there might be something strange going on is this sentence: "[T]he defendant was arrested the following day by officers investigating reports of a 'tall, distinctive-looking man' connected to a series of break-ins at flats in Swansea's Maritime Quarter."

In order for a reader to understand that this violent perpetrator is a man, he or she would have to first think, "I wonder if this article is actually referring to a man" and proceed to research that question. But that defies common sense. People do not typically read a news item and wonder whether the reporter is simply lying about something as central as the sex of a violent offender. But if a reader did research the question, they would learn that Victoria is, in fact, a man.[42]

There are a few important takeaways here. One is that each example above (and countless others) provides concrete evidence of the abolition of sex in journalism; it is not only happening in the law. Another is that we are all being lied to and—in the classic definition of the term—abusively gaslit by the media. We are being told that violent crimes are committed by women when that is simply not true.

Reporting on crime is one thing; recording it is another. In the U.S., the FBI has been publishing crime statistics since 1930 through a program called the Uniform Crime Reporting System (UCR) which receives crime data from local law enforcement and compiles it into various tables. Table 42 contains the FBI's reporting on arrests by sex.[43] It is clear from the data that males commit

---

41   Jason Evans, "Woman puts on hi-vis jacket to burgle key workers' hotel in Swansea," Wales Online (December 10, 2020).

42   Trans Crime UK, "Victoria Midrange" (December 17, 2020).

43   FBI: UCR, "2019 Crime in the United States," Table 42, https://ucr.fbi.gov/crime-in-the-u.s/2019/crime-in-the-u.s.-2019/topic-pages/tables/table-42.

the overwhelming majority of crime, especially violent and sex crime. For example, in 2019—the most recent year for which data is currently available—males committed 88 percent of murders, 97 percent of rapes, 84 percent of robberies, and 77 percent of aggravated assaults. The only category in which a majority of perpetrators are female is prostitution, which is not surprising. Women appear to have slightly higher rates of embezzlement, and the only other crime category in which women come even close to men in terms of arrest rate is larceny (theft).

How might President Biden's "Executive Order on Preventing and Combating Discrimination on the Basis of Gender Identity or Sexual Orientation" affect the FBI's ability to track crime statistics in the future? Readers may remember that this order, entered on January 20, 2021, requires all federal agencies to redefine sex to include "gender identity" in their policies and regulations. Presumably, because the FBI is within the Justice Department and is therefore clearly an executive agency, it will have to comply with this directive.

On June 28, 2021, a group of twenty-one state (plus Washington D.C.) attorneys general called upon the Justice Department to do just that. In a letter to U.S. Attorney General Christopher Wray, these state officials urged him to "act swiftly to add a non-binary gender designation to its Uniform Crime Reporting."[44] Their argument in favor of taking such action is that because local law enforcement agencies submit their crime data to the FBI using the UCR system, they encounter errors when they try to submit data regarding so-called "non-binary" individuals because the system does not permit the entry of a "non-binary gender." As for what "non-binary" may mean, the letter simply states that "[i]ndividuals whose gender is not male or female commonly use the term 'non-binary' to refer to their gender identity."

At this point, we must ask: Why on earth would our society want to track crime statistics based on an ill-defined word that

---

44   Attorney General Letter (June 28, 2021) 1. https://www.nj.gov/oag/newsreleases21/Uniform-Crime-Reporting-Letter-From-21-State-AGs-on-Non-Binary-Gender-Designation.pdf.

some people may use to "refer to their gender identity?" Does that do anything to help us prevent and deter crime? Does it help us understand crime patterns? More importantly, *how will we as a society be able to confront the reality of male violence against women if we cannot record and report accurate data about the sex of perpetrators?* We do not do this with any other identity category. Why would do it with "gender identity?"

Another area in which our society has not fully thought through the consequences of abolishing sex is in medicine and public health research. Very often, health care professionals need to know which sex a person is in order to administer safe and effective health care. A competent gynecologist would not administer a cervical screening test on a man, and a competent urologist would not treat a woman for a prostate infection for obvious reasons.[45] Male and female bodies are simply different in ways that matter, medically. We know, for example, that sex affects the functions of the human immune system.[46]

If we abolish sex, what will happen to our ability to conduct necessary public health research? According to the National Institutes of Health:

> "Women now account for roughly half of all participants in NIH-supported clinical research, which is subject to NIH's Policy on the Inclusion of Women in Clinical Research. However, more often than not, basic and preclinical biomedical research has focused on male animals and cells. An over-reliance on male animals and cells may obscure understanding of key sex influences on health processes and outcomes.

---

45   Though, inexplicably, some have argued that men who claim to be women can get cervical cancer and therefore should visit a gynecologist. Canadian Cancer Society, "Trans women and cervical cancer screening," https://www.cancer.ca/en/prevention-and-screening/reduce-cancer-risk/find-cancer-early/screening-in-lgbtq-communities/trans-women-and-cervical-cancer-screening/?region=qc.

46   Sabra L. Klein and Katie L. Flanagan, "Sex difference in immune responses," Nature Reviews Immunology 16, 626–638 (2016).

Accounting for sex as a biological variable begins with the development of research questions and study design. It also includes data collection and analysis of results, as well as reporting of findings. Consideration of sex may be critical to the interpretation, validation, and generalizability of research findings. Adequate consideration of both sexes in experiments and disaggregation of data by sex allows for sex-based comparisons and may inform clinical interventions. Appropriate analysis and transparent reporting of data by sex may therefore enhance the rigor and applicability of preclinical biomedical research."[47]

Acknowledging the material reality of sex *matters* for our society's ability to engage in this type of research.

Let's take a hypothetical example to illustrate this point. Let's say that a drug company is conducting a clinical trial of a new drug that has the potential to cure prostate cancer and is offering $500 to men who are willing to participate. I sign up on the basis of my supposed "male gender identity." Remember, in a world where "gender identity" reigns supreme, the fact that I do not have a prostate is irrelevant; all that matters is that I claim to "identify as a man." Under a legal regime that protects "gender identity" for all purposes, the drug company would be discriminating against me on the basis of "gender identity" if it were to deny my participation in the trial. After I sign up, I complete all the necessary paperwork, ticking the box for "M," and proceed to take the experimental drug. The drug company then tests the effects of the drug on my body and incorporates the results into its research. The company reports that all testing on men has been completed with positive results, and the drug is eventually approved. Would the men who later take the drug to cure their

---

47   National Institutes of Health, Office of Research on Women's Health, "NIH Policy on Sex as a Biological Variable," https://orwh.od.nih.gov/sex-gender/nih-policy-sex-biological-variable.

prostate cancer even know that at least one of the test participants was female? Wouldn't they have the right to? Shouldn't they?

If readers think this sounds preposterous, that's because it is. *And yet, in a world where sex is abolished at the altar of "gender identity," there is no reason whatsoever that this could not happen or even become commonplace.*

The above examples illustrate that the abolition of sex has grave consequences for all of society which very few people have even begun to think through. However, the most devastating impacts are being, and will continue to be, experienced by women and girls.

The Prisoners' Dilemma

There are men, many of whom have been convicted of extremely violent and sexual offenses, including rape and murder, being housed in women's prisons. We do not know the exact number, but it is likely in the hundreds.[48] In some states, like Washington, this is because sex has been abolished as a matter of state administrative policy; in other states, like California, it is because sex has been abolished as a matter of state law.

The California state legislature enacted SB 132 in 2020, and it went into effect in January 2021. The law codified the existing policy of the California Department of Corrections and Rehabilitation (CDCR) to house inmates in accordance with their self-described "gender identity." According to the state's legislative digest's summary of the law:

> "This bill would require the Department of Corrections and Rehabilitation to, during initial intake and classification, and in a private setting, ask each individual entering into the custody of the department to specify the individual's gender identity whether the individual identifies as transgender, nonbinary, or intersex,

---

48   The U.S. chapter of the Women's Human Rights Campaign is, at the time of writing, collecting data to document the exact number and the nature of their offenses of conviction.

and their gender pronoun and honorific. The bill would prohibit the department from disciplining a person for refusing to answer or not disclosing complete information in response to these questions. The bill would authorize a person under the jurisdiction of the department to update this information. The bill would prohibit staff, contractors, and volunteers of the department from failing to consistently use the gender pronoun and honorific an individual has specified in verbal and written communications with or regarding that individual that involve the use of a pronoun or honorific.

The bill would require the department, for a person who is transgender, nonbinary, or intersex to only conduct a search of that person according to the search policy for their gender identity or according to the gender designation of the facility where they are housed, based on the individual's search preference. The bill would additionally require the department to house the person in a correctional facility designated for men or women based on the individual's preference, except as specified."[49]

There is no mention, or even recognition, of the material reality of sex. No consideration is given to the safety of either the women in prison or the female correctional officers who are presumably going to be required to conduct intimate searches of male inmates. California lawmakers enacted this law, which ignores the fact that women are a coherent class of people who deserve rights, privacy, and safety, and the governor signed it.

---

49   California SB 132, Legislative Counsel's Digest, https://leginfo.legislature.ca.gov/faces/billTextClient.xhtml?-bill_id=201920200SB132.

Women in prison, the majority of whom have not committed a violent offense, are often themselves victims of physical and/or sexual abuse, and many of them struggle with addiction. A disproportionate number of these women are black or Latina. These women are terrified. An attorney with the Women's Liberation Front recently posted a recording of herself speaking with a woman in a California prison, who stated: "The sad part is, when we come to our staff members and we say, 'What do we do? We're fearful. We don't wanna live with them... What's gonna happen if they try to abuse us, and our roommates don't want to get involved?' And it's just heartbreaking because the response she gets, the response I get, the response our peers get, is 'Oh, you know how to scrap, you know how to fight, defend yourself.'" [50]

In July 2021, it was reported that CDCR had begun posting signs related to anticipated pregnancy in the women's prison and handing out condoms to inmates. According to the Women's Liberation Front, "[t]he new resources are a tacit admission by officials that women should expect to be raped when housed in prison with men, where all sex is considered non-consensual by default within the system."[51] WoLF is right, of course, that CDCR *was* anticipating rape, as all sex *is* considered non-consensual within the system, as it must be. In addition, CDCR officials know who among its inmate population has HIV, but it is not entirely clear whether any of the male prisoners that California is transferring to the women's prison are HIV-positive. [52] Are California prison officials handing out condoms to female inmates not only as way to prevent pregnancy, but also to prevent HIV transmission?

Furthermore, for California to provide pregnancy information and condoms to female prisoners is a tacit admission by the state that the men who are being transferred into women's prisons are *not women*. If they were, by definition, pregnancy would not be a concern. The state *knows* that it is transferring men into women's

50   Women's Liberation Front, "Incarcerated Woman Speaks Out on the Impact of SB 132 (July 6, 2021).
51   Women's Liberation Front, "CA Women's Prisons Anticipate Pregnancy After Forcing Women to be Housed with Men," Women's Liberation Front (July 15, 2021).
52   Barrett Newkirk, "California prisons see benefit in routine HIV testing," Desert Sun (February 26, 2016).

prisons. This blows a hole right through the claim that is often put forth that "transwomen are women." We all know that is not true. What kind of woman is capable of getting another woman pregnant with her body? A woman with a penis and testicles? But this is the logic of "gender identity"—a logic that is being peddled by irresponsible lawmakers and spread throughout the media.

Washington state does the same thing, as a matter of administrative (Department of Corrections) policy. On March 10, 2021, it was reported on a local radio program that an anonymous employee of the state prison system contacted the station to expose the fact that "a half dozen men" had been transferred to the women's facility.[53] Allegedly, two of the men who are being held in the prison are Donna (Douglas) Perry, who was previously convicted of serially murdering prostituted women, and Princess Zoee Marie Andromeda Love (whose real name is Hobby Bingham), who was previously convicted of raping a twelve-year-old girl.

This story has received no known national mainstream media attention, but the Women's Liberation Front reports that a woman, on her own, filed a public records request with the state to obtain information about these individuals. After she filed this request, the ACLU and an organization called Disability Rights Washington filed a lawsuit to block the state from responding. That request was partially granted. Although the court prevented the state from revealing any *identifying information* of any of the male inmates who were being housed in the women's facility, it did permit the state to reveal the *number* of such individuals. The responsive documents show that there are seven inmates who "identify as female, non-binary, or any other gender identity that are currently housed in a women's facility."[54]

That this story is receiving no nationwide attention is astonishing. While there has, to date, been no official systematic effort

---

53   Dori Monson, "DOC employee reports men are claiming to be women to transfer prisons," KIRO Radio (March 10, 2021).

54   Women's Liberation Front, "Confirmed: Ruling in Washington ACLU Reveals Male Rapists Housed in Women's Prisons," Women's Liberation Front (May 19, 2021).

to track these scenarios nationwide, thanks to women's organizations that are compiling the data via FOIA requests and webpages such as Women are Human, Ovarit, and This Never Happens, we do have some information about the men who are being housed in women's prisons across the U.S. on the basis of their so-called "female gender identity."

We know, for example, that in Alabama, there are three men being housed in women's prisons and that their convictions include sex offenses involving children and attempted murder. In Alaska, the only man being housed in a women's prison was convicted of theft. In Arizona, there are six men being housed in a women's prison whose crimes include sex offenses involving children, negligent homicide, murder, assault, bestiality, and fraud. The story is similar in other states across the country. It appears that the only states that do not currently have any men in women's prisons on the basis of their supposed "gender identity" are Delaware, Hawaii, Mississippi, New Hampshire, Rhode Island, and South Dakota.[55]

The only reason that prison officials are able to house men in women's prisons is by disregarding the reality of sex, and the reason that this is possible is that lawmakers—either legislatively or as a matter of policy—have abolished sex in the law for this purpose by declaring that inmates are to be housed on the basis of their "gender identity." Women are the casualties.

The Invasion of Women's Sports

Women's sports have turned out to be of tremendous benefit to women and girls in myriad ways. It has been shown, time and again, that when girls compete athletically, they tend to go on to strive for success academically and professionally and have greater self-confidence than they otherwise might have.

---

55   On file with author. Many thanks to Robin Cohen for compiling all of this information and for permitting me to use it here.

The overwhelming majority of Americans agree that sports should be separated by sex.[56] And yet, over and over again, we are seeing women and girls being forced to compete with and against men and boys on the basis of the boys' so-called "gender identity" because most states have laws and policies on the books that abolish sex for the purpose of assigning athletic team membership. Starting in 2019, and gaining steam in 2020 and 2021, Americans started to push back and introduced bills in various states that are designed to keep sports single-sex. The reason that bills like these are necessary is that across the country, we are seeing scenarios, such as the one that arose in Connecticut discussed in Chapter 2, in which men and boys are being permitted to participate in women's sports on the basis that they claim to "identify as women."

This is not limited to high school athletics. June Eastwood is a man who formerly competed on the women's cross-country team at the University of Montana and would go on to compete in an NCAA's Division 1 race.[57] Chelsea Wolfe is a man who beat several women in the trials for the U.S. BMX women's 2021 Olympic team.[58]

Nor is the situation limited to the United States. Laurel Hubbard is a man who won the right to compete on the New Zealand women's Olympic 2021 weight-lifting team because he satisfies the International Olympic Committee's (IOC) rules regarding testosterone suppression.[59] The current IOC policy allows men to compete in women's Olympic sports if they had declared their "gender identity" as female for at least four years and could demonstrate that their testosterone level is below 10 nanomoles per liter for at least one year, and Hubbard satisfies those criteria. However, notwithstanding this sexist policy, it should not need to be said that "female" is not a "gender identity" or that a woman

56   Women's Liberation Front, National Poll Reveals Majority of Voters Support Protecting Single-Sex Spaces," Women's Liberation Front (October 27, 2020).

57   Jeff Welsch, "While fighting HB 12, transgender former UM runner Juniper Eastwood finds clarity on trails," 406 MT Sports (February 14, 2021).

58   Alex Raskin, "BMX rider Chelsea Wolfe becomes Team USA's first transgender Olympian after qualifying for Tokyo Games as an alternate," Daily Mail (June 18, 2021).

59   Julia Hollingsworth, "A transgender weightlifter's Olympic dream has sparked an existential debate about what it means to be female," CNN (July 4, 2021).

is not simply a man with a self-declared identity and lower than average male testosterone levels. Hubbard did go on to compete in the Olympics and lost. When the women who did medal in gold, silver, and bronze gave a news conference after the competition, they were asked if they wanted to comment on Hubbard's participation. After a long pause, U.S. weightlifter Sarah Robles replied, simply, "No thank you." It was painfully obvious that she did not approve of Hubbard's participation.

Veronica Ivy (formerly Rachel McKinnon, formerly Rhys McKinnon) is a man who competes in women's cycling. He is a Canadian academic who, in 2019, took the world record in women's cycling.[60] Previously, in 2012, he had earned his Ph.D. in philosophy with a thesis titled, "Reasonable Assertions: On Norms of Assertion and Why You Don't Need to Know What You're Talking About."[61] Hannah Mouncey is a man who competes in Australian women's handball.[62] Valentina Petrillo is an Italian runner who competes in women's track.[63] He once insultingly said of his dominance in Italian women's running, "better to be a slow happy woman than a fast unhappy man."[64] Examples like these abound all over the world.

There have been multiple efforts at the state level to protect women's and girls' sports for women and girls. As of writing, thirty-seven states had introduced such bills through 2021. Even though a majority of Americans support the separation of sports by sex, nearly all of the support for this legislation comes from Republican lawmakers. Very few Democratic lawmakers have had the courage to stand up for women and girls at the state or federal level. There is a strong case to be made that standing up for women's and girls' sports should not be left to Republicans. Title IX was a huge feminist victory, and it is extremely unfortunate that today, its only outspoken defenders are political conservatives.

---

60   Canadian Cycling, "Transgender world champion Rachel McKinnon defends title in Manchester," (October 22, 2019).

61   Rhys McKinnon, Reasonable Assertions: On Norms of Assertion and Why You Don't Need To Know What You're Talking About (University of Waterloo 2012).

62   Cyd Zeigler, "Hannah Mouncey says teammates pushed her away over locker room use," Out Sports (August 28, 2020).

63   Karleigh Webb, "Italian sprinter Valentina Petrillo chases a Tokyo dream," Out Sports (July 10, 2020).

64   Dany Mitzman, "Valentina Petrillo: 'Better to be a slow happy woman than a fast unhappy man," BBC News (June 4, 2021).

It is well-established that men retain a competitive advantage over women in sports. Testosterone suppression does not ameliorate this fact. [65] This truth is grounded in science and backed up by common sense. It is the reason we have sex-specific athletics in the first place. But even if that were not true, shouldn't women have the right to say no to men? Why do most liberals champion women's right to say no to men in the bedroom but not on the playing field?

It is often argued that we should accommodate the boys and men who claim to be girls and women into female-only sports because there are so few of them and allowing them to compete is a kind thing to do. But the simple truth, which we must acknowledge if we are being honest, is this: If we allow even one man or boy to compete on a team that is reserved for women and girls, we must allow men and boys to take over women's sports completely. This is true both practically and logically.

As a practical matter, a women's team of any sport that has boys or men participating is going to be at an advantage, and as such teams win because of that advantage, coaches and administrators are going to start recruiting more and more boys and men onto their teams in order to retain their competitive edge. Further, as a logical matter, if we are going to allow one man or boy to compete on a girls' or women's team, there is no reason not to let men and boys take over completely. If there is a limit to the number of men and boys that we are going to allow to compete as women or girls, what is that limit, and whatever that limit is, why?

Shelters

In 2018, a Toronto woman who was also a sex abuse survivor was living in a shelter for addiction recovery when she was told that she would be required to share a room with a pre-operative "transwoman."[66] When she complained to the Ontario Human Rights Legal Support Centre, she was told that *she* was the one who was engaging

---

65   Emma Hilton and Tommy R. Lundberg, "Transgender Women in the Female Category of Sport: Perspectives on Testosterone Suppression and Performance Advantage," 51 Sports Medicine 2, 199-214 (2021).

66   Joseph Brean, "Forced to share a room with transgender woman in Toronto shelter, sex abuse victim files human rights complaint," Toronto National Post (August 2, 2018).

in discrimination because she had referred to the person as a man. After two traumatic nights of being required to share a room with him, she left and became homeless.

This has happened in the U.S. as well, going at least as far back as 2013, when two women in Portland, Maine complained that two men had been admitted to a shelter that was meant to house women exclusively, using the same common bathrooms, showers, and sleeping facilities.[67]

In June 2021, a homeless shelter in Anchorage, Alaska sued the city regarding its policy mandating that single-sex shelters and similar facilities permit men to be housed in accordance with their female "gender identity."[68] The complaint alleges violations of the Free Exercise Clause of the First Amendment, the Free Speech Clause of the First Amendment, Freedom of Expressive Association, Freedom of Private Association, and Due Process.

As discussed above, this is now official U.S. federal administrative policy—domestic violence shelters that receive federal funding are prohibited from "discriminating against" people on the basis of "gender identity."[69] What this means in practice is that all over the country, if a man wants to be housed in a women-only *domestic violence* shelter, all he has to do is declare that he is a woman. Again, we are referring here to shelters whose very purpose is to house women who are escaping abusive domestic situations.

Lesbian Erasure and "Woke Homophobia"

As bad as the situation is for women and girls generally, it has created a particularly devastating environment for lesbians who, by definition, do not seek to have romantic or sexual relationships with

---

67   Joe Lawlor, "Transgender clients at Portland women's shelter draw complaints," Portland Press Herald (July 15, 2013).

68   Emily Goodykoontz, "Faith-based Anchorage women's shelter sues city over changes to LGBTQ anti-discrimination law," (June 3, 2021).

69   Tracy Jan, "Biden administration withdraws Trump-era proposal to allow homeless shelters to discriminate against transgender people," *Washington Post* (April 22, 2021).

men. Time and again, I have been told by lesbian feminists that they are fed up with being told that if they do not wish to date biological males, they have a bigoted and hateful "genital preference." Indeed, the very concept of women being solely attracted to women is being relegated to the dustbin of history.

Merriam-Webster defines a lesbian as "a woman who is sexually or romantically attracted to other women."[70] This is common sense for most of us. Whatever readers may think about homosexuality and(or) marriage equality, we all understand the concept—lesbians are women who are sexually or romantically attracted to other women. It is not complicated. However, as discussed in Chapter 1, the very definitions of the words "woman" and "women" appear to be up for debate today. If that is true, is the definition of the word "lesbian" up for debate as well? When asked, most lesbians will say, "No, of course not." And yet, tragically, these definitions actually *are* being debated.

When I was in my early thirties, I spoke with a woman—I'll call her Olivia—about her experience of understanding that she was a lesbian. Olivia told me that one day, when she was fifteen years old, she was playing basketball in a mixed-sex group of friends. She had always known that she was different from other girls and had zero sexual or romantic interest in boys, but it had not yet occurred to her that she was a lesbian. That day, while she was playing basketball, she just knew. She stopped playing and stood in the middle of the court, thinking, "Oh. I'm attracted to girls. That means I'm a lesbian." She came out shortly thereafter and never once dated or had any kind of sexual relationship with a man or boy. She has had her share of relationship ups and downs, of course, but all of her relationships were with women, i.e., adult human females. That was never in question. I have not spoken with Olivia in several years, but the last time I was in communication with her, she was happily married and living with her wife and their children.

---

70   Merriam Webster, "Lesbian," https://www.merriam-webster.com/dictionary/lesbian.

It is much more difficult to discuss topics like this openly today. I was once speaking with an older lesbian, the mother of a teenage girl who was confused about whether she was actually a boy or a girl. This mother had come out of the closet as a lesbian in rural Texas in 1979. She is politically very liberal and has liberal and progressive friends. Although her friend circle was completely accepting of her relationship with her wife, she found it much more difficult to have open conversations with friends about her daughter's struggle with "gender identity." She told me that it was *easier* for her to come out as a lesbian in rural Texas in 1979 than it was to talk with her liberal and progressive friends about "gender identity" today.

In 2019, a young radical feminist lesbian named Julia Beck served as co-chair of the legal and policy committee of the Baltimore "LGBTQ Commission," a body established to advise the mayor and other city officials on "LGBTQ" policy in the city.[71] During committee meetings, Beck refused to refer to men (so-called "transgender women") as "she" and "her." At one point, she referenced the case of Karen White, a male prisoner in the UK who was housed in a women's prison on the basis of his "gender identity" and went on to sexually assault two female inmates.[72] Beck said during a committee meeting that she would not refer to this male rapist as "she." The committee then voted her out of her leadership position, leaving no out lesbians on the committee.

If one hangs out in radical feminist circles for any length of time, one will learn a lot about the thriving lesbian culture of the '60s, '70s, and '80s, about women-only spaces, and women-only events and land. All those things are disappearing upon the insistence of men who claim to be women and the society that enables them. MichFest (the Michigan Womyn's Music Festival) was an annual gathering of women, mostly lesbians, from 1976 to 2015. It was intended to be exclusively for women, and it received a lot

---

71   Jean Marbella, "Baltimore lesbian's view on transgender women gets her kicked off LGBTQ panel – and onto Tucker Carlson Show," The *Baltimore Sun* (February 14, 2019).

72   Nazia Parveen, "Karen White: how 'manipulative' transgender inmate attacked again," The *Guardian* (October 11, 2018).

of criticism for excluding men (so-called "transgender women"). It eventually shuttered in 2015, after sustaining years of abuse from a group that called itself "Camp Trans"—men who objected to MichFest's women-only policy.[73]

One active participant in "Camp Trans" was Dana Rivers. Rivers was born David Warfield. In 1999, he claimed that he was a woman and underwent surgery to persuade others that he was, in fact, a woman. At the time, he was a high school teacher. He openly discussed his fetish with his teenage students and was subsequently fired. He sued, and the case was settled.

Just after midnight on November 11, 2016, police received reports of gunshots being fired at a home on Dunbar Drive in Oakland, California. When they responded, they found Rivers drenched in blood and running from the doorway of the house. He was in possession of knives, ammunition, and metal knuckles. The house was on fire. Inside, the police found two women whose bodies were riddled with bullets and stab wounds. These were Patricia Wright and Charlotte Reed, a married lesbian couple. Police also found a young man laid out in front of the house who had been shot to death—this was Toto Diambu (known as Benny Diambu-Wright), their nineteen-year-old adopted son. Rivers has been charged with numerous serious and violent offenses, including murder and arson. The trial has been continued numerous times while the court awaits a report regarding Rivers' mental health.

I spoke with one woman, a lesbian who has been out for over forty years (who wishes to remain anonymous) about the impact of "gender identity" on lesbians' lives and communities. She said, "For lesbians, there is obviously the loss of our spaces and things like that. But the thing that's most horrifying is rape. Fortunately, these guys don't force huge numbers of lesbians into having sex with them, but things are getting more and more heavy-handed and there are starting to be more and more women who have no other social circle who *are* being coerced. So, like I said, aside

---

73   Lauren Levey and Marian Rutigliano, "Michfest, a celebration," The Glinner Update (April 21, 2021).

from the loss of our spaces (we can still meet privately with other lesbians), today men just expect to be able to have sex with us or unspeakably harass us. It's rape."

Increasing numbers of lesbians, gay men, and bisexual people (LGB) are taking a stand against the inclusion of the "T" in the acronym. In this connection, it is important to understand that sexual orientation and "gender identity" are not remotely the same thing, although they are typically linked together via the acronym "LGBT." Sexual orientation is about sexual attraction to people of the same sex, the opposite sex, or both sexes, whereas "gender identity" is a fiction that denies the reality of sex altogether.

In order to truly understand the impact that the "gender identity" movement is having on lesbians and bisexual women, I reached out to an organization called LGB Fight Back, which advocates for the interests of the LGB community. Their website states, "We promote self-love and radical self-acceptance among homosexual and bisexual men and women, because we're perfect just the way we are."[74]

LGB Fight Back's members have identified three major areas in which the "gender identity" movement is fundamentally at odds with LGB rights and undermines the interests of lesbians and bisexual women.

1. *Lesbians are pressured to have unwanted sex with men who claim to be women.*

    •   "The pressure on lesbian and bisexual women to accept male 'lesbians' into our dating pool is astounding," said the National Organizer of LGB Fight Back, Carrie Hathorn. This phenomenon, called the "cotton ceiling" by "gender identity" ideologues, is seen as a new form of homophobia by members of the LGB community. As one member puts it: "Twenty years ago, men would say 'rape her straight' or 'you'll like it if you try it.' The only thing that's changed is that they found a way to make it accept-able. They call us bigots just for having sexual boundar-ies." LGB Fight Back calls this "woke homophobia."

- "It's impossible to use lesbian dating apps now," anoth-er woman writes. "They're full of 'trans lesbians,' a.k.a. straight men ... if you tell them you're not interested, they bully you, call you vile names like 'vagina fetishist,' and make violent threats. I've been avoiding 'lesbian' events altogether because I don't want to come face-to-face with these homophobic men. It's terrifying."

- Other members spoke out about their fears of being sub-jected to male violence from so-called "trans lesbians" like Dana Rivers, the man who, at the time of writing, stands accused of murdering lesbian couple Patricia Wright and Charlotte Reed, along with their son: "Every time my girl-friend speaks out against trans ideology, I'm afraid we're going to be next ... I'm constantly sick with anxiety that something is going to happen to one or both of us just because we don't believe that men can be lesbians."

- "Trans ideologists have created a terrorist culture where lesbians have to go back in the closet or live in fear," an-other member concluded.

2. *Lesbians and bisexual women, particularly those who don't con-form to sex-based stereotypes, are pressured to undergo dangerous medical procedures in order to "transition."*

    - According to LGB Fight Back's members, the medicaliza-tion of lesbians has left gaping holes in the lesbian community. "Of all the lesbians I knew in high school and college," one member tells me, "I'm the last one left who's not calling herself a man."

- For both LGB Fight Back's National Organizer and Research Coordinator, the issue of lesbian erasure hits close to home. Carrie tells the story of a lesbian friend who got caught up in "gender identity" ideology and took testosterone and had her breasts removed in order to appear as a straight man. "We keep hearing that transing saves lives," Hathorn says, "but my friend's attempt to live 'authentically' didn't save her life." Carrie's friend committed suicide in 2018 at the age of thirty-one.

- LGB Fight Back's Research Coordinator, who wishes to remain anonymous, has also seen her fair share of lesbians claiming to be "trans men," including her first love. She explained the pain of having to pretend that Jenna had been "Lenny" all along: "'Lenny,' the fictional person Jenna created for herself to hide behind, trumped everything real—her name, her sex, the history of the homophobia leveled against us both, and my right to tell my own story and call myself a lesbian." (Names have been changed to protect individuals' privacy.)

- LGB Fight Back has called the "transing" of LGB people Medical Conversion Therapy. "Teens and 20-somethings obsess over 'gender identity,'" writes the Research Coordinator in another email, "and they take same-sex attraction as a sign that they're actually 'trans.'"

- "When Ellen Page transed herself, I thought, *another lesbian down*," Carrie said. "It's not so much about Ellen herself, but what she represents… lesbian erasure." LGB Fight Back is concerned about the influence this will have on young lesbians: "It's a blow to the whole community to lose another lesbian to transgenderism. And Page has become a walking advertisement for medicalization. We are really concerned that more young lesbians will follow suit."

- Another member writes, "It's a big pyramid scheme where lesbians are conned into taking testosterone as a solution for all of their problems, and then influence other lesbians to do the same. The medical establishment, the pharmaceutical industry, and Big Psych are profiting by putting lesbians into a medical closet. It's a medical scandal in the making."

3. *The lesbian and bisexual female community has lost the freedom to gather, socialize, and organize without male intrusion.*

- LGB Fight Back is a multi-generational organization, so they've watched the destruction of the lesbian community from different vantage points. But they all agree that the lesbian community has all but disappeared. One lesbian who grew up in the '80s writes: "When I was a teenager, I discovered the local gay newspapers. I was amazed to see people just like me in the pages … the community was vibrant. But that community is gone now. We have no spaces just for ourselves anymore."

- Hathorn, who is in her forties, says, "The Gay and Lesbian community centers and organizations we used to rely on no longer serve us. The absence of community, including role models, makes young lesbians vulnerable to Big Pharma's instant-gratification advertising schemes. A whole generation of LGB people have been miseducated and pushed into medical conversion therapy."

- A lesbian in her twenties agrees: "By the time I was ready to come out, I couldn't even find any other lesbians. When I complained about it to my therapist, she asked whether I knew of any lesbian dating apps where her 'trans woman' clients could meet lesbians to 'validate' their identities. Does she really think lesbians are validation machines for men? I've been painfully lonely my whole adult life, and even my therapist doesn't care."

- "It's like they don't want lesbians and bisexual women to be able to meet each other," another member wrote. "So many lesbians are isolated because of gender ideology. Without community, we lack a social support system, and our mental health suffers. The lesbian community was virtually the only area in our lives where we didn't face bigotry and homophobia."

When I speak with lesbians, gay men, and bisexual men and women, it is clear that transgenderism is fundamentally at odds with the legal rights and social acceptance of LGB people. There is nothing wrong with having a same-sex attraction, and all of "transgender" ideology obscures that reality. My hope in including their voices here is that readers will understand the impact of the "gender identity" industry on LGB people. I am immensely grateful to the members of LGB Fight Back who shared their insights and concerns with me.

The simple fact is that all of this follows inevitably from the abolition of sex in law and policy. Our society simply cannot protect anyone on the basis of sex—women and girls, including lesbians, especially—if we ignore that it exists. This situation is nothing but devastating for women and girls, and for lesbians in particular.

We could list countless examples of the ways in which women and girls are disproportionately impacted by the abolition of sex. I discussed public accommodations (bathrooms, locker rooms, and so forth) previously in Chapter 2 (with regard to the implications of passing the Equality Act) and an incident in Los Angeles where a spa was allowing nude men to have access to the women's section. A similar situation occurred in Washington D.C. in 2019 when Charlotte (née Charles) Clymer accessed the women's restroom of a popular restaurant.[75] When staff asked to see identification to confirm that Clymer is a woman, Clymer took the restaurant before the D.C. Human Rights Commission and won. The restaurant was ordered to pay a fine of $7,000 to the city as punishment and the staff member who confronted Clymer was fired.

Until Americans across the political spectrum take a stand against the abolition of sex, this is going to continue. One part of the difficulty here is that these topics are very difficult to talk about in today's climate. The next chapter explores that topic.

---

75   Justin Wm. Moyer, "D.C. restaurant fined $7,000 after asking transgender woman for ID before letting her use bathroom," *Washington Post* (January 17, 2019).

Chapter 4:

The Abolition of Sex in Media and Discourse

THE TOPICS I HAVE BEEN DISCUSSING are not generally permitted to be talked about in public. When words like these are spoken, the speaker is often labeled "hateful" and "bigoted" or sometimes "racist," "fascist," or "Nazi." Explanations for these accusations are rarely provided. The closest anyone has ever come to justifying the accusation of racism is that insisting on single-sex bathrooms mirrors Jim Crow racial segregation. But this is ridiculous. Men and women are different for the purpose of using the restroom in ways that people of varying racial backgrounds are not different for that purpose. I have heard it said that "sex is a social construct that was imposed on others through colonialism and eugenics." But this statement is *itself* profoundly racist. Those who take this position are essentially arguing that the people of the global south (Africa, East and South Asia, and South America) had no idea how babies are made before Europeans came along to inform them. Beyond that, though, explanations for these kinds of accusations are rarely given. The women and men who acknowledge biological reality are simply given these labels, and society seems to tolerate such behavior.

This is just the tip of the iceberg. The entire English language is being manipulated and twisted in order to obscure the reality of sex. In June 2021, the Biden administration replaced the word "mothers" with the words "birthing people" in a section of a budget proposal regarding infant mortality.[76] In a guide on "Safer Sex for Trans Bodies," the Human Rights Campaign urges readers to refer to a vagina as a "front hole" and to a penis as a "strapless."[77] In July 2021, the Centers for Disease Control issued some guidance related to the COVID-19 pandemic and the risk of illness, stating: "Although the overall risk of severe illness is low, pregnant people and recently pregnant people are at an increased risk for severe illness from COVID-19 when compared to non-pregnant people."[78] This is ridiculous, as we all know that even though not all women get pregnant, everyone who gets pregnant is a woman. But, as we saw earlier in Chapter 1, women are being told that we are "transphobic" simply for stating that a woman is an adult human female.

In this chapter, we will address three of the primary areas in which women (and some men) who speak about these matters are silenced: (1) the news media and social media, (2) cancellation and deplatforming, and (3) the law. The chapter concludes with some thoughts about the modern phenomenon of "preferred pronouns" and a discussion about "preferred pronoun" mandates.

Media and Social Media

Most of the mainstream U.S. news media has never provided any honest coverage of the feminist critique of "gender identity." Whenever the mainstream media covers any story related to sex and gender, the coverage is biased. It is so biased, in fact, that it uses words like "trans" and "transgender" with the apparent assumption that everyone knows what those words mean, that they are uncontroversial, and that there is a coherent and shared definition of them.

---

76   John Kass, "Why are we calling mothers 'birthing persons'?" The *Baltimore Sun* (June 21, 2021).
77   Human Rights Campaign, "Safer Sex for Trans Bodies," (June 8, 2015).
78   Centers for Disease Control, COVID-19, "Pregnant and Recently Pregnant People," (July 3, 2021).

Consider a few recent headlines:

- *Wave of Bills to Block Trans Athletes Has No Basis in Science, Researcher Says*[79]

- *The bans on transgender athletes—6 facts*[80]

- *Federal Government Reinstates Health Care Protections for Transgender Americans*[81]

When headlines use the phrases "trans athletes" and "transgender athletes," they are almost always referring to men and boys, but virtually no mainstream media outlet will say that. When they refer to "health care" for "transgender" people, they mean puberty blockers, cross-sex hormones, and surgeries that result in sterility and disease, but virtually no mainstream media outlet will say it. To most Americans, these headlines probably sound straightforward; in truth, they are anything but.

When the media does cover feminist perspectives on sex and gender, it invariably does so in a way that casts feminists as "conservative" when in reality, so-called "gender identity" is grounded in regressive stereotypes about what boys and men are like versus what girls and women are like, and actual feminists almost never think of themselves as being "conservative" or "right-wing." Though I have not conducted a survey, it is probably safe to say that all of the feminists I know personally, or have studied, have political views that are grounded in classical left-wing values and ideology.

In January 2019, three members of the Women's Liberation Front appeared on a panel at the conservative Heritage Foundation. The panel was titled "The Inequality of the Equality Act:

79   Tinbete Ermyas and Kira Wakeam, "Wave Of Bills To Block Trans Athletes Has No Basis in Science, Researcher Says," NPR (March 18, 2021).
80   Zoe Christen Jones, "The bans on transgender athletes – 6 facts," CBS News (June 7, 2021).
81   Corinne Lewis, "Federal Government Reinstates Health Care Protections for Transgender Americans," The Commonwealth Fund Blog (May 11, 2021).

Concerns from the Left."[82] The speakers were Jennifer Chavez, Julia Beck, me, and Hacsi Horvath, a lecturer at the Department of Epidemiology and Biostatistics at UC-San Francisco, and a man who once claimed to be a woman. All four of us considered ourselves to be on the political left, and we shared our concerns about the Equality Act in similar ways.

The event received very little mainstream media attention, naturally enough (although it did get quite a bit of coverage in conservative media). NBC covered it, though, under the revealing headline, "Conservative group hosts anti-transgender panel of feminists 'from the left.'"[83]

There is a very good reason we agreed to do this panel at Heritage: No other entity would have us. I know a mother who worked for years to find a left-leaning or non-partisan think tank in Washington to host a discussion of left-leaning concerns about the Equality Act and about the harmful effects of giving young people puberty blockers and/or cross-sex hormones and surgeries. All of them turned her down. Finally, in desperation, she asked me if I could reach out to the Heritage Foundation on behalf of WoLF. I said yes to this desperate mother, and I have no qualms about it.

But back to the NBC headline: One might ask why the phrase "from the left" is set in quotation marks. Does the author question whether the panelists were actually leftists? The answer is yes. It has become the norm to frame *all* critique of "gender identity" as coming from the political right. If a feminist speaks up about the importance of protecting the rights, privacy, and safety of women and girls, she will therefore be labeled "right-wing."

One media outlet, the *Washington Post*, covered an event hosted by the Women's Liberation Front in 2020 at the Seattle Public Library (SPL).[84] In the months leading up to the event, many called upon the SPL to cancel it, referring to it as encouraging "harmful rhetoric toward a community that is already mar-

---

82   The Heritage Foundation, "The Inequality of the Equality Act: Concerns from the Left," (January 28, 2019).
83   Tim Fitzsimons, "Conservative group hosts anti-transgender panel of feminists 'from the left,'" NBC News (January 29, 2019).
84   Video of the event can be found on YouTube, here: https://www.youtube.com/watch?v=voaYjKMw5rI. The video is the property of the Women's Liberation Front.

ginalized and endangered."[85] SPL had several regular meetings, during which this issue was discussed at length, and the library appeared to be seriously considering the calls for cancellation. In the end, the event went forward over the objections of those who oppose free speech for women.

To her credit, Samantha Schmidt at the *Washington Post* at least covered the event.[86] To the best of my knowledge, this is the only time that any U.S.-based mainstream media outlet has ever covered a radical feminist event taking place on U.S. soil. Unfortunately, however, the piece did not cover WoLF's arguments fairly or accurately. Schmidt reports: "The Women's Liberation Front is part of a long-running strain of feminism that rejects the existence of transgender ideology." That is not true—the members of WoLF are (painfully) well-aware that the ideology exists. It's also somewhat amusing that she acknowledges that it's an ideology because proponents of the ideology consistently argue, without providing any credible evidence, that there is science to back it up. She accuses WoLF of "helping to bolster" a Republican message, which is also untrue—WoLF advances a *feminist* message, not a Republican one. Not a single speaker on the panel at the event was a Republican, and two of the speakers were not even American.

It is true that most media outlets that are willing to publish feminist voices in this debate are conservative-leaning. Some of them include Fox News, the *National Review*, the *Washington Examiner*, the *New York Post*, the *Daily Signal*, and the *Federalist*. There are a couple of reasons for this. One is that having feminists speak out against "gender identity" helps advance a genuine shared interest in protecting female-only spaces. Another is that feminists simply cannot get a hearing in mainstream media outlets, and when we do, the coverage distorts our message and paints us as conservative. Feminists are regularly criticized for appearing on conservative-leaning media outlets—and I understand why. I get this kind of reaction

85   Megan Burbank, "Despite criticisms from LGBTQ community, Seattle Public Library will allow 'radical feminist' event to proceed," (January 10, 2020).

86   Samantha Schmidt, "Conservatives find unlikely ally in fighting transgender rights: Radical feminists," *Washington Post* (February 7, 2020).

every time I appear on Tucker Carlson's Fox News show. However, our critics do not seem to understand that if MSNBC or NPR would give us a platform, we would be more than happy to take it.

The social media scene is no better. Posting feminist content has gotten numerous women, and a few men, suspended from Twitter and banned from Facebook. As noted earlier, Canadian journalist Meghan Murphy (editor in chief of The *Feminist Current*), comedy author Graham Linehan, and Kellie-Jay Keen Minshull have all been permanently banned, as have been numerous lesser-known feminists and male friends.

On December 19, 2019, *Harry Potter* author J.K. Rowling famously tweeted: "Dress however you please. Call yourself whatever you like. Sleep with any consenting adult who'll have you. Live your best life in peace and security. But force women out of their jobs for stating that sex is real? #IStandWithMaya #ThisIsNotADrill."

Rowling was referring to Maya Forstater, a British tax expert who previously engaged in contract work with the Center for Global Development. Forstater's work focused on international development and had nothing whatsoever to do with sex or gender. However, in her spare time, and under her own name, she had tweeted that men are male and referred to a man wearing a dress as "a man in a dress." Subsequently, her employer chose not to renew her contract. Forstater sued and lost. In its ruling, the tribunal overseeing the matter held that Forstater's views were "not worthy of respect in a Democratic society." She appealed and prevailed. The appellate body ruled that, in fact, Forstater's views are protected under established U.K. law.

Meanwhile, Rowling's tweet was met with immediate calls for her rape, death, and cancellation. Millions of former fans announced that they intended to burn their copies of *Harry Potter and the Sorcerer's Stone* as punishment for her heresy. Rowling has been the target of literally thousands of vile and disgusting tweets. There are too many examples to reiterate, but here are a few:[87]

---

87   These were shared on Twitter by a user named "Dataracer" (@dataracer117) and can be found here: https://twitter.com/Dataracer117/status/1272737061703790592.

"This woman is complete scum. Shut the fuck up you transphobic fuck. You don't know or love any trans people if you won't even acknowledge their existence. Thanks for ruining the books of my childhood. Just stop talking."

"@jk_rowling die"

"The j.k. stands for 'just kill.'"

"JK Rowling die b*tch."

"@jk_rowling bitch I'll kill you."

Rowling received more online abuse in July 2021, when she tweeted: "To be fair, when you can't get a woman sacked, arrested or dropped from her publisher, and cancelling her only made her book sales go up, there's really only one place to go." This was in response to someone who had tweeted, "I wish you a very nice pipebomb in mailbox."

Threats of violence in response to statements about sex and gender that ought to be completely innocuous have become routine.

The Facebook experience is similar. People (mostly women, but some men) are routinely suspended for various periods of time or told that their comments violate amorphous "community standards" (often colloquially referred to as being in "FB jail"). Typically, the content is a factual statement like, "Women don't have penises." I asked a few people who had been subjected to this type of treatment to provide documentation. Here are some examples of what they reported:

"I was told that posting an actual CBS story about 'questionable hysterectomies' violated community standards."

> "I got a 3-day suspension for voicing con-
> cerns about gay conversion therapy."

> "I got a 30-day suspension for saying that
> humans can't change sex."

In short, it appears to be the consensus of the mainstream media and of every social media platform that dissenting feminists are not allowed to speak about women's rights separate from men.[88]

The reason for this bias is not mysterious. Nearly all mainstream media outlets follow the AP Stylebook, which is painfully confusing on these topics. Its reference to "sex" in the Index simply states, "See gender." Its reference to "gender" states: "Not synonymous with sex. *Gender* refers to a person's social identity while sex refers to biological characteristics. Not all people fall under one of two categories for *sex* or *gender*, according to leading medical organizations, so avoid references to *both*, *either*, or *opposite* sexes or genders as a way to encompass all people." It encourages the use of "cisgender" to refer to "people who are not *transgender* in stories about gender, as a means to distinguish people from one another," and defines "transgender" as "an adjective that describes people whose gender identity does not match the sex or gender they were identified as having at birth." Nowhere does the AP seek to define "gender identity."[89]

The reason feminists are regularly banned or suspended from social media platforms is not mysterious either. Facebook's community standards prohibit "objectionable content," which includes what is deemed (by Facebook itself) to be "hate speech." From Facebook's community standards page:

> "We define hate speech as a direct attack
> against people—rather than concepts or insti-
> tutions—on the basis of what we call protected

---

88   Dozens of additional examples are available on file with the author.
89   The Associated Press, "Stylebook 2019 and Briefing on Media Law," The Associated Press (2019).

characteristics: race, ethnicity, national origin, disability, religious affiliation, caste, sexual orientation, sex, *gender identity* [emphasis added] and serious disease. We define attacks as violent or dehumanizing speech, harmful stereotypes, statements of inferiority, expressions of contempt, disgust or dismissal, cursing and calls for exclusion or segregation. We also prohibit the use of harmful stereotypes, which we define as dehumanizing comparisons that have historically been used to attack, intimidate, or exclude specific groups, and that are often linked with offline violence."[90]

Again and again, when "gender identity" (which no one can define with any clarity) is protected, women are silenced, and our rights trampled on.

Twitter also has a policy regarding allegedly "hateful conduct," which is quite extensive.[91] It states, among other things:

> "You may not promote violence against or directly attack or threaten other people on the basis of race, ethnicity, national origin, caste, sexual orientation, *gender, gender identity*, religious affiliation, age, disability, or serious disease. We also do not allow accounts whose primary purpose is inciting harm towards others on the basis of these categories." (Emphasis added.)

Notably, Twitter does *not* prohibit promoting violence against, directly attacking, or threatening other people on the basis of *sex*—which is presumably why it allows tweets that directly promote violence against, directly attack, or threaten women.

---

90   Facebook, "Community Standards: Objectionable Content," https://business.facebook.com/communitystandards/objectionable_content.

91   Twitter, "Help Center: Hateful Conduct Policy," https://help.twitter.com/en/rules-and-policies/hateful-conduct-policy.

Clearly, in most jurisdictions, inciting or promoting violence is unlawful; so to that extent, Twitter's policy makes complete sense. The question of what constitutes a "direct attack," however, is questionable. I recently asked one former Twitter user (a man who supports feminists in this cause and used Twitter primarily for that purpose) what, exactly, he said that got him banned. He responded that he doesn't even know because no offending tweet was provided. In other words, Twitter is banning users who post feminist content without telling them what about it constitutes a "direct attack."

Twitter's policy also states:

> "**Hateful imagery and display names**: You may not use hateful images or symbols in your profile image or profile header. You also may not use your username, display name, or profile bio to engage in abusive behavior, such as targeted harassment or expressing hate towards a person, group, or protected category."

But it never tells us what it means by "hateful." In contemporary society (and as we will see below, in law), it is generally considered "hateful" to say that women don't have penises because, according to "gender identity" ideology, some women in fact have penises. But why is it "hateful" to question this? We do know that Twitter prohibits "targeting individuals with repeated slurs, tropes or other content that intends to dehumanize, degrade or reinforce negative or harmful stereotypes about a protected category. This includes targeted misgendering or deadnaming of transgender individuals." It remains a mystery why saying that women don't have penises violates this policy.

Also worth pointing out is that Twitter prohibits "[e]ncouraging others to commit violence against an individual or group based on their perceived membership in a protected category, e.g., 'I'm in the mood to punch a [BLANK], who's with me?'" Yet people often say exactly this when threatening to punch or kill "TERFs." Feminists are routinely threatened with death, rape, and assault, as we saw in the case of J.K. Rowling.

The mainstream media simply will not permit feminists to talk about our rights *as women* because doing so is deemed to be "offensive" or "hateful." The mainstream media keep us out by simply refusing to platform us. When we try to speak out on social media, we are subjected to punishments—usually suspensions in the case of Facebook and either temporary or permanent bans in the case of Twitter. The abolition of sex has become so entrenched in our society that we are not even allowed to talk about it using traditional modes of communication.

Cancellation and Deplatforming

I have already discussed the WoLF Seattle Library event in February 2020. Not only did our opponents try to persuade the library to cancel our event, some of them attended and interrupted it with shouts of "TRANSPHOBE!" and "YOU ARE HORRIBLE PEOPLE!" They let off piercing air horns and stomped their feet. Eventually, the police had to be called, and the offenders were forcibly removed to loud chants of "LET WOMEN SPEAK!" We were finally able to proceed with the event. Meanwhile, hundreds of protestors gathered outside, yelling and holding signs that read "FUCK TERFs," and punching the glass windows of the library. After the event, the speakers had to be ushered through this mob by security guards; as they tried to drive away, protestors pounded on the roof and hood of the car.

This type of thing is not even slightly unusual. In 2020, Oxford University professor Selina Todd was scheduled to speak at an event titled the Oxford International Women's Festival, but her invitation was withdrawn at the last minute due to complaints of "transphobia."[92] Holly Lawford-Smith is an Associate Professor in

---

92   BBC News, "Oxford University professor condemns exclusion from event," (March 4, 2020).

Political Philosophy at the University of Melbourne. In November 2020, she was kicked off the writing platform Medium for critiquing "gender identity" (she had already been banned from Twitter because she opposes the abolition of sex in Australia).[93]

Another tactic proponents of "gender identity" use is trying to get women terminated from their jobs or otherwise reprimanded for wrongthink. Earlier this year, some of Lawford-Smith's detractors—a mixture of UM students, staff, and people outside the University—complained about a website she created to document personal stories about the "impacts on women of men using women-only spaces, including but not limited to: changing rooms, fitting rooms, bathrooms, shelters, rape and domestic violence refuges, gyms, spas, sports, schools, accommodations, hospital wards, shortlists, prizes, quotas, political groups, prisons, clubs, events, festivals, dating apps, and language."[94] Lawford-Smith's detractors claimed that her actions "contributed to an atmosphere of transphobia on campus and in wider society" and demanded the University take "swift and decisive action." [95] Others have protested her lecturing on feminism and demanded that her courses be cancelled.[96]

Donna Hughes is a professor at the University of Rhode Island who has written about ways in which the fantasy that sex is not real is a bit similar to the ways in which groups like QAnon fantasize about political developments such as the notion that Donald Trump won the 2020 Presidential election.[97] After receiving complaints, university administrators publicly reprimanded her.[98]

Callie Burt is a professor of criminology at Georgia State University and a feminist. In June 2020, she published an article titled, "Scrutinizing the U.S. Equality Act 2019: A Feminist Examination of Definitional Changes and Sociolegal Ramifications," in which she presented arguments similar to the ones I

---

93   Holly Lawford-Smith, "The Digital Deplatforming of a Gender Critical Feminist," (November 23, 2020).
94   No Conflict They Said, https://www.noconflicttheysaid.org/ (Currently administered by LGB Alliance Australia.)
95   Karl Quinn, "'Transphobic' website puts Melbourne University academics at odds," *Brisbane Times* (February 25, 2021).
96   Holly Lawford-Smith, "Censorship Timeline," Holly Lawford-Smith, https://hollylawford-smith.org/censorship-timeline/.
97   Donna M. Hughes, "Fantasy Worlds on the Right and Left: QAnon and Trans-Sex Beliefs," 4W (February 28, 2021).
98   Colleen Flaherty, "At Odds With her University Over Gender Identity," (March 25, 2021).

outlined in Chapter 2. In April 2021, she was removed from the editorial board of a publication called Feminist Criminology amid accusations that she is "transphobic."[99]

Kathleen Lowrey is an associate professor of anthropology at the University of Alberta in Canada. She is also a signatory to the Declaration on Women's Sex-Based Rights (described below). She had taken on the departmental position of associate chair of undergraduate programs at the start of the 2019-2020 school year. At the beginning of the year, she told students that she intended to introduce materials that had fallen out of favor in academia. By this, she meant feminist critiques of gender. She also had signs up in her office indicating her support for women's sex-based rights. Later, in March 2020, she was told that she was no longer "effective" in her role and was being terminated from that position. The administration refused to provide a written explanation, but the reasons were made clear in a conversation that she had (and recorded with permission) with her department chair and faculty dean.[100]

These examples pertain to women who are being cancelled from academic positions; but as dire as the situation is in academia, it is not limited to that realm.

Anna Kerr is an Australian attorney who founded The Feminist Legal Clinic in Sydney, whose mission is to advance the human rights of women and girls. Most of its focus centers on representing domestic violence victims, but it also advocates for women's sex-based rights. The clinic operated out of a site operated by the City Council. But in June 2021, the clinic was informed that its status was being downgraded and that its lease was being terminated due to its overt support for women's sex-based rights.[101]

Sasha White is an American woman who was fired from her position with a literary agency for tweeting: "TW [trans women]

99   Callie Burt, "Context of my Removal from the Editorial Board of Feminist Criminology," Callie Burt (April 23, 2021).

100   Jeff Labine, "U of A professor says she was dismissed over views that biological sex trumps transgender identity for policy decisions," *Edmonton Journal* (June 9, 2020). Also on file with author.

101   Sky News Australia, "Sydney Lord Mayor downgrades feminist legal clinic," (June 24, 2021).

being vulnerable to male violence does not make you women."[102] On July 15, 2021, two female educators at an Oregon middle school—one an assistant principal and one a 7th-grade teacher— were fired from their jobs.[103] The two women had previously advocated for a campaign called "I Resolve," which they described as an effort to create a safe environment for all children, including the maintenance of sex-specific restrooms and the teaching of biological sex in the school curriculum.

While studying law at the Abertay University in Dundee, Scotland, Lisa Keogh made the seemingly innocuous statement that women have vaginas. As a consequence, she faced disciplinary action at the hands of school administrators but was later cleared of wrongdoing.[104] After the initial disciplinary action was taken, the matter was addressed by the U.K.-based television outlet LBC, which invited U.K. Member of Parliament Liz Truss to appear. The anchor asked Truss for her thoughts, and she replied, simply, "Women do have vaginas, Nick."[105] This is where we are as a society today. Sex has been abolished to the point that Members of Parliament have to go on national television to explain that yes, in fact, women have vaginas, in defense of a female law student who faced disciplinary action for having the temerity to say so.

Efforts to silence women are not new, of course. "Gender identity" is simply a modern-day version of the scold's bridle, which was used for centuries throughout Europe and North America to silence and punish women who had the gall to talk too much.

---

102   Jo Tweedy, "New York literary agent who 'stands with J K Rowling' is fired for retweeting comment that read, 'being vulnerable to male violence does not make you a woman' on her personal Twitter account," *Daily Mail* (August 25, 2020).

103   M.K. Fain, "Two Oregon Educators Fired After Speaking Out About Gender Identity Policies," 4w.pub (July 17, 2021).

104   Maggie Baska, "Scottish law student faces disciplinary action over 'women have vaginas' row," Yahoo News (May 19, 2021).

105   LBC, "Liz Truss 'Women do have vaginas, Nick" (May 30, 2021), https://www.youtube.com/watch?v=DELcVItEkrE.

Using the Law to Silence Women

The First Amendment protects Americans from being punished by the government (any level of government) for our speech. That law is not absolute, and some exceptions are permitted—most of us are familiar with the clear and present danger doctrine, for example. But for the most part, we permit unpopular speech in the U.S.

However, we are starting to see cracks in our collective commitment to free speech in the U.S. New York City law "requires employers and covered entities to use the name, pronouns, and title (e.g., Ms./Mrs./Mx.) with which a person self-identifies, regardless of the person's sex assigned at birth, anatomy, gender, medical history, appearance. Or the sex indicated on the person's identification."[106] It goes on to note, "[m]ost people and many transgender people use female or male pronouns and titles. Some transgender, non-binary, and gender non-conforming people use pronouns other than he/him/his or she/her/hers, such as they/them/theirs or ze/hir. They/them/theirs can be used to identify and refer to a single person." This has potentially dire First Amendment implications.[107]

In other countries, the situation is even more dire. Scotland has had a "hate speech" law on the books since 1986 when it made "stirring up hatred" on the basis of race unlawful. In May 2021, it added age, disability, religion, sexual orientation, "transgender identity" and variations in sex characteristics to the list of covered categories. However, it is not entirely clear what "stirring up hatred" means, nor is it obvious what a "transgender identity" is. A cursory review of the literature suggests that "stirring up hatred" can include "some form of threatening, abusive or insulting words, behaviour, material, images or sounds."[108] Clearly, people

106   New York City Human Rights Commission, "Gender Identity/Gender Expression: Legal Enforcement Guidance, https://www1.nyc.gov/site/cchr/law/legal-guidances-gender-identity-expression.page#3.1.

107   Eugene Volokh, "You can be fined for not calling people 'ze' or 'hir' if that's the pronoun you demand that you use," *Washington Post* (May 17, 2016).

108   Scottish Government, "HATE CRIME AND PUBLIC ORDER (SCOTLANE) BILL INFORMATION NOTE, https://www.gov.scot/binaries/content/documents/govscot/publications/factsheet/2020/04/hate-crime-bill-what-it-will-do/documents/hate-crime-bill-stirring-up-hatred-offences/hate-crime-bill-stirring-up-hatred-offences/gov-scot%3Adocument/Hate%2BCrime%2BBill%2B-%2BInformation%2BNote%2BPdf%2B-%2BStirring%2BU-p%2BHatred%2BOffences%2B-%2BRevised%2BAugust%2B2020.pdf

should not be threatening each other, but Scotland already criminalizes "threatening or abusive behavior,"[109] as it should. Women who critique "gender identity" ideology are frequently told that our words are "insulting"—should that really be a crime?

Marion Millar is a Scottish feminist who works with an organization called For Women Scotland, which advocates for Scottish women's sex-based rights. She is also a working mother. In June 2021, she was charged under Scotland's existing hate speech law (not the new law, which had not yet taken effect).[110] Her alleged offense? A tweet containing an image of a suffrage ribbon. That's right. A woman tweeting an image of a suffrage ribbon is apparently so offensive, so terrifying to some people, that Scottish law enforcement felt justified in *charging her with a crime* (the complainant argues that the ribbon is arranged in such a manner that it resembles a noose). It appears that in some places, celebrating the fact that women are allowed to vote may constitute "stirring up hatred" under national criminal law.

The reason this was seen as so offensive is apparently that Millar believes women deserve rights on the basis of our sex. Today, women are being arrested and charged with criminal offenses for holding such beliefs. To express this belief constitutes heresy, socially and under the law in some places. Notably, the hashtag #WomenWontWheesht took off on Twitter some time ago, and women are still using it. "Wheesht" is Scottish vernacular for "shut up" and #WomenWontWheesht is a sentiment I am more than happy to applaud, even if it eventually lands me in jail.

There are numerous such "hate speech" laws in place all over the world, most of them punishing speech advocating violence and/or genocide against particular groups of people. Whatever one thinks of the validity of "hate speech" laws in general, and there are reasonable arguments on both sides of the debate, such laws should

---

109　Crime.scot, "Threatening or Abusive Behaviour – Criminal Justice and Licensing (Scotland) Act 2010 s38," https://crime.scot/s38/.

110　Libby Brooks, "Gender-critical feminist charged over allegedly transphobic tweets," The *Guardian* (June 4, 2021).

not, under any circumstances, criminalize words that women (and men) use to raise critiques of "gender identity" ideology.

Even though there are no "hate speech" laws on the books in the U.S., I am aware of at least one example where a U.S. woman has been charged with a crime on the basis of conduct that constitutes speech. On Friday, September 24, 2021, a woman named Thistle Pettersen was charged with the offense of disorderly conduct under Wisconsin state law, with an additional charge that the offense constituted a hate crime. The original complaint stated:

> "The above-named defendant on or about Saturday, July 17, 2021, in the City of Madison, Dane County, Wisconsin, while in a public place, did engage in violent, abusive, indecent, profane, boisterous, unreasonably loud and/or otherwise disorderly conduct, under circumstances in which such conduct tended to cause a disturbance, contrary to sec. 947.01(1), 939.51(3)(b), 939.645(1) and (2)(b) Wis. Stats., a Class B Misdemeanor, and upon conviction may be fined not more than One Thousand Dollars ($1,000), or imprisoned not more than ninety (90) days, or both.

> And further, invoking the provisions of sec. 939.645(1) and (2)(b) Wis. Stats., because the defendant committed a crime under chapters 939 to 948, and selected the property that is damaged or otherwise affected by the crime in whole or in part because of the defendant's belief or perception regarding the sexual orientation of the owner or occupant of that property, the penalty increase under this section changes the status of the crime to a felony and the re-

vised maximum fine is $10,000 and the revised
maximum term of imprisonment is 2 years."

The complaint was subsequently amended to clarify that the hate speech enhancement elevated the underlying offense to a more serious misdemeanor, not a felony.

Pettersen's alleged offense was placing a sticker with the words "TERF Collective" on a media box located in a public area. "TERF Collective" refers to a loosely affiliated group of radical feminists who have decided to "reclaim" the TERF label by putting it on themselves rather than allowing their enemies to use it as an insult.

During a hearing the following Monday, the complaint was dismissed on First Amendment grounds, but that Pettersen faced criminal charges *with a hate crime enhancement for the alleged offense of stickering a feminist message in a public area* is utterly chilling.

We have to be able to say what sex is and what it is not. We have to be able to critique the abolition of sex in the law. We must vigilantly protect our right to speak the truth.

The Tyranny of Pronouns

We live in an era of "preferred pronouns." What this means is that in many business, educational, employment, and social contexts, people are expected (and sometimes required) to introduce themselves with their "preferred pronouns." Typically, this involves announcing whether one prefers to be referred to as "she/her," "he/him," or "they/them" (consistent, presumably, with whatever "gender identity" they are experiencing at any given moment). But some people state that they prefer other pronouns, such as fae/faer, ve/ver, or xe/xem. This linguistic denial of actual sex is being promoted by otherwise reputable colleges and universities, like Duke University, the University of Wisconsin, Springfield College, and many others, in a deliberate attempt to obscure reality.[111]

---

111   *See, e.g.,* Duke University Student Affairs Center for Sexual and Gender Diversity, "Gender Pronouns Resource Guide," https://studentaffairs.duke.edu/csgd/training-resources/gender-pronouns.

This is completely ridiculous, as any thinking person knows. And yet, some people seem to take it very seriously, including Vice President Kamala Harris, who as a presidential candidate introduced herself at a Town Hall discussion in October 2019 by first stating her preferred pronouns.[112] This was obviously not necessary, as everyone on the face of the planet understands that Kamala Harris is a woman, and therefore female. The moderator, then New York Governor Andrew Cuomo's brother Chris, acknowledged as much when he jokingly responded, "Mine too." A chastened Cuomo later apologized. Clearly to some people, this is no laughing matter.

The idea that we are all required, in any context, to announce our "preferred pronouns," as though the reality of biological sex is not completely obvious, demonstrates the extent to which our society will go to deny material reality. I have personally experienced this phenomenon on several occasions. The most egregious instance was at a professional conference on criminal justice reform. I was attending a panel presentation on police militarization not long after the events in Ferguson, Missouri. After the panel presentations, the facilitator invited anyone in the audience who wanted to ask a question to stand, state his or her name, organizational affiliation, and "preferred pronouns." I had a question that I thought would contribute helpfully to the discussion. I knew, however, that if I stood to speak without providing my "preferred pronouns," I would be asked for them. Refusing to state them under these circumstances would have meant professional ruin. So I remained seated and kept my mouth shut.

This is how social conformity works, and how people can silently assent to the most absurd propositions imaginable. Indeed the more absurd they are, the less likely they are to be challenged.

In July 2021, San Francisco District Attorney Chesa Boudin announced that "preferred pronouns" would become a matter of

---

112   Ian Schwarz, "Kamala Harris: 'My Pronouns are She, Her, and Hers'; Cuomo: 'Mine too,'" Real Clear Politics (October 10, 2019).

official policy.[113] Under the new mandate, prosecutors and others will be *required* to ask witnesses *and defendants* about their "identifying pronouns." The DA's office is a government entity, and it is not at all clear whether this policy complies with the First Amendment, which prohibits compelled speech under certain circumstances. For example, in *West Virginia State Board of Education v. Barnette*, the U.S. Supreme Court ruled that a school board's policy of requiring students to state the Pledge of Allegiance constituted an unconstitutional "compulsion to declare a belief."[114]

Whether the District Attorney of San Francisco may lawfully compel his attorneys to declare a belief in "gender identity" by mandating the use of "preferred pronouns" is an interesting question. Whether the policy can survive a First Amendment challenge is especially interesting—if any employee has the courage to bring one, which seems doubtful. At least one federal court has ruled that criminal courts are under no obligation to use a defendant's preferred name or pronouns, although that court did not rely on the First Amendment in doing so.[115] It is also not clear how a female rape victim will feel about having to refer to her male alleged rapist as "she" if he claims to be a woman. One wonders whether Boudin has given any thought to this sensitive matter.

It's not all bad news on the free speech front. In February 2019, Nicolas Meriwether filed a case in federal court in Ohio, where he works as a philosophy professor at Shawnee State University (a public institution).[116] Between 2016 and 2019, he had a series of interactions with a student and school administrators that led him to file the lawsuit. It is his preferred pedagogical style to address students as "Mr." or "Ms." when asking and responding to questions. At the beginning of the 2016–2017 school year, an unnamed male student demanded to be addressed as "Ms." and referred to using "she/her" pronouns. Professor Meriwether

---

113   Lawrence Richard, "San Francisco district attorney mandates city officials to use preferred pronouns," Washington Examiner (July 3, 2021).
114   *West Virginia State Bd. of Educ. v. Barnette*, 319 U.S. 624 (1943).
115   *U.S. v. Varner*, 948 F.3d 250 (2020).
116   Adam Carrington, "In Transgender Case, the Sixth Circuit Understood How the First Amendment Protects the Conditions Needed for a Good Education," Real Clear Education (April 7, 2020).

refused. Over the course of the next several years, Meriwether offered numerous compromises that would permit him to address the student in a manner that respected the student's chosen identity *without* being forced to declare that the student was female (something his religious convictions prohibited him from doing).

None of these compromises was acceptable, however, and university administrators ultimately formally disciplined him. Meriwether sued and lost at the lower court level, but he eventually won when the 6th Circuit Court of Appeals ruled that he had a First Amendment free speech right, as well as a right to religious liberty, not to be compelled to use wrong-sex titles or pronouns. That ruling remains good law for now.

That our language has changed so dramatically as to make the natural, material reality of sex nearly invisible, with so little public debate, is astounding. And yet, the abolition of sex in language, as in law and the media, is occurring so rapidly that it is difficult to discern. It has simply happened right before our eyes. Again, although this hurts everyone, it harms women and girls in particular. If we cannot talk about sex, we cannot talk about sexism. If we cannot talk about sexism, we cannot fight back against it. If we cannot fight against it, we will never achieve liberation. We are all on the losing end of this, but women and girls have the most to lose. If we do not take a stand, we will lose it all, for certain.

Chapter 5

The Gender Identity Industry

WHY IS THIS HAPPENING? Why are all three branches of the U.S. government abolishing sex in the law? Why are women being forced to cede ground to and share spaces with men under the false pretense that they are female? Why are we not permitted to talk about this? Why are the media—which includes many smart and powerful women—misleading and gaslighting us? Why are women losing their jobs for stating that sex is real? I am asked these questions frequently.

An invisible industry exists that is driving this entire apparatus, and although it operates openly, few people seem to know about it. Its primary objective is simple but breathtakingly audacious: to obliterate human life as we know it. The philosophical starting point for this radical campaign is the denial of nature and the limits it places on our ability to reimagine ourselves and the world. Only by dethroning the idea of objective reality and asserting the primacy of subjectivity—i.e., "lived experience"—can we create a new reality of godlike freedom in which all have the ability to remake themselves in their own projected image. Women's rights and interests, to the extent that they depend on our biological existence as women, are obstacles in the way of this agenda. Obliterating biological sex in the law and throughout society is thus the starting point. Women's rights and bodies are collateral damage.

The "gender identity" industry is grounded in a vicious blend of woman-hatred, science-denial, and greed. This statement may seem shocking or outlandish. Bear with me as I explain.

In 1979, University of Massachusetts, Amherst, Professor Janice G. Raymond published a prophetic book called *The Transsexual Empire: The Making of the She-Male*, in which she predicted everything that occurred in the realm of transsexualism (and transgenderism, which we could call transsexualism 2.0) over the subsequent forty or so years.[117] Raymond noted that "transsexualism" is an ideology that is not grounded in material reality in the sense of *actually* changing sex or "being born in the wrong body," and argues that "*[t]ranssexualism at this point constitutes a "sociopolitical program" that is undercutting the movement to eradicate sex-role stereotyping and oppression in this culture.* Instead it fosters institutional bases of sexism under the guise of therapy" (emphasis in original).[118]

Raymond locates her discussion of these matters within the realm of morals, values, and ethics. She appears to be less interested in debating the veracity of the claim that people can change sex (although she makes it clear that the answer is *no*) than in discussing the ways in which transsexualism harmfully reinforces sex-role stereotypes. She is widely and accurately credited with being one of the first feminists to do so. In short, she saw this all coming, and she warned us.

It is extremely tempting to dismiss all of this as a fringe conspiracy. No one *wants* to truly understand the extent or the gravity of what is happening to women in this country under the guise of tolerance and inclusivity. Acknowledging the truth behind the movement to abolish sex is painful and difficult to even get our minds around. However, it is all operating in plain sight

---

117   Janice Raymond, "The Transsexual Empire: The Making of the She-Male," (Beacon Press 1979), reprinted in 1994 with a new Introduction on transgenderism by Teacher's College Press (Transsexual Empire).
118   Transsexual Empire at 5.

once we open our eyes to it. If we do not reign in the "gender identity" industry, the complete legal and social abolition of sex will be accomplished.

What is the "gender identity" industry? As stated previously, it is a loose conglomeration of businesses, law firms, medical and pharmaceutical companies, governments, media outlets, universities, and non-profit organizations that are engaged in a conspiracy to lie to all of us about what is happening.[119] By this, I do not mean to suggest that there is a conspiracy in the traditional legal sense of an overt agreement among these parties, but rather in the sense that there is, generally, a tacit agreement among some of the most powerful entities in our society to persuade everyone that sex does not exist as a material reality and that subjective identity is supreme.

All of this began to emerge in the '60s and '70s in U.S. academic institutions with the propagation of post-modern thought, which morphed into "queer theory." So-called "queer theorists" actively promote the notion that biology is socially constructed and that we can escape it by simply "identifying" out of it. One contemporary American "queer theorist" is Judith Butler, Maxine Elliot Professor in the Department of Comparative Literature and the Program of Critical Theory at the University of California, Berkeley. Butler's work builds, in turn, on the work of Michel Foucault, a twentieth-century philosopher who argued for reductions in, and sometimes elimination of, the age of consent in rape laws.

According to philosopher Susan Cox:

> "Queer theory is very much influenced by Michel Foucault, who is called the father of queer theory. He really popularized this method of what he calls "historical genealogy." He originally got it from Nietzsche, but he popularized it in the 20th century as a part of postmodernist thought. So he performs these

---

119   The 11ᵗʰ Hour Blog is indisputably the best source of information on this. www.11thhourblog.com.

historical genealogies, for example history of madness, history of sexuality; to show how homosexuality became seen as deviant.

And this is an important thing to do. But what queer theory does is it takes power out of the equation and says that these norms happen almost by chance, which is also from Foucault. Foucault argued that these norms kind of happen through contingency. And contingency is basically chance. They just sort of form that way, they just get momentum for some reason and keep going. No one knows quite why and they don't really benefit any specific group of people.

Similarly, Judith Butler said that women are not oppressed for the benefit of males, but that these norms simply come to be and that they are very restrictive and oppress people in that fashion."[120]

According to queer theory, then, women are not oppressed by men on the basis of sex, but on the basis of the existence of the binary category of sex. This is fundamentally anti-feminist. More to the present point, queer theorists talk frequently about *queering the binary*. A good example of this appears here:

Butler (1990, 1993) influentially argued that our biology is not a neutral base upon which gender is culturally constructed. As shown by Laqueur (1990) and others, even our bodies are culturally constructed in that they are understood in culturally specific ways. Ac-

---

120   Resistance Radio Transcripts, "Susan Cox 1.28.17," (January 28, 2017).

cording to Butler (1990, p. 10), "perhaps this
construct called 'sex' is as culturally constructed as gender; indeed, perhaps it was always already gender, with the consequence that the
distinction between sex and gender turns out
to be no distinction at all."[121]

So-called queer theory, with its insistence that bodies are
"culturally constructed," is the beginning of the end of the material reality of sex—it all follows directly from that.

But how did an obscure (and non-sensical) academic theory
go from the Ivory Tower to everyone's living rooms, classrooms, and
boardrooms, and throughout the law itself? I would argue that once
the academy succeeded in "queering the sex binary," three things happened that would create the necessary conditions for the contemporary abolition of sex in law and throughout society: (1) the inven-
tion of the word "transgender;" (2) the explosion of corporate-driven
technologies and medical practices; and (3) the thorough embrace of
the sexual exploitation of women and girls on the political left.

If someone had tried to sell Americans the idea that sex isn't real
by quoting some harebrained scheme cooked up by a handful of off-
the-wall academics, it never would have succeeded. Everyone, after
all, knows how babies are made. In order to accomplish the goal of
persuading Americans to go along with the pretense that sex doesn't
exist, we needed a new word. That magic word is "transgender."

As discussed in Chapter 1, this word has no coherent meaning
whatsoever. And yet its enshrinement in society's lexicon has done a
tremendous job of persuading most of us that it does. It is tempting
to think that there is a political divide regarding the acceptance of
"transgender people," but that is misleading. It is facile, though understandable, to think that people on the political left are "tolerant"
or "accepting" of "transgender people" and that people on the political right are "intolerant" or "unaccepting" of them because this is the

---

121   James Aimers, "Queering the Sex and Gender Binary," Chapter 4: Queer New World: Challenging Heteronorma-
         tivity in Archaeology, in LGBTQ+ Studies: An Open Textbook, ed. Deborah Amory and Sean Massey (SUNY 2020).

way that the matter is always framed in the media. But it is not true. It is true that in the U.S., Democrats are behind the push to enshrine "gender identity" in the law and that many Republicans oppose it. But most Republicans, rank-and-file and leadership alike, even while opposing the enshrinement of "gender identity" in the law, still accept that "transgender" is a coherent category of people. I am here to assure them it is not.

The word "transgender" is simply a linguistic sleight of hand whose purpose is to persuade everyone that sex does not exist. Unfortunately for all of us, it has largely succeeded in accomplishing that objective.

Raymond addresses the word "transgender" in her Introduction to the 1994 republication of *The Transsexual Empire*. It is a fascinating glimpse into the original imposition of the word "transgender," and it is mandatory reading for anyone who is concerned about how "transgender" harms women and girls. In a section on "The Politics of Transgenderism," Raymond writes: "The issue of transsexualism has been largely superseded by debates over transgenderism or what has been called 'sexuality's newest cutting edge.' The term, transgender, covers preoperative and postoperative transsexuals, transvestites, drag queens, cross dressers, gays and lesbians, bisexuals, and straights who exhibit any kind of dress and/or behavior interpreted as 'transgressing' gender roles."[122] This does indeed seem to be the case, although, as discussed above, since 1994 it also seems to be the case that a person can "be transgender" simply by announcing that one "is transgender." If "transgender" means everything, it means nothing.

Raymond goes on to describe all of the ways in which "transgender," like "transsexual" and other terminology often used to mean some form of adopting stereotypical sex roles, does absolutely nothing to challenge the political reality—men have political power and women do not. She also discusses the challenges that many lesbians must navigate in

---

122　*Transsexual Empire*, 1994 Introduction, xxv.

the difficult world where women are generally expected to behave in stereotypically "feminine ways," and she examines the nature of "gender bending," or, as some might call it today, "gender nonconformity."

She concludes, "The ideal of transgender is provocative. On a personal level, it allows for a continuum of gendered expression. On a political level, it never moves off this continuum to an existence in which gender is truly transcended. Its supposedly iconoclastic rebellion against traditional gender confinement is more style than substance. What good is a gender outlaw who is still abiding by the law of gender?"[123] Her predictions have all come true—"transgender" IS more style than substance, and it does nothing to subvert the very real world in which women remain a political sub-class.

But it has proven to do even more damage than anyone predicted—not only has it succeeded in reinforcing the sex-role stereotypes that have always existed; it has succeeded in persuading virtually all of society that sex *itself* does not exist. That one little word has accomplished so much more than the queer theorists ever would have been able to accomplish, sitting in their ivory towers and preaching to the converted about "queering the binary."

The insertion of the word "transgender" into our lexicon has not accomplished all of this on its own, however. It has been supported and fueled by corporate interests that constantly insert themselves into our daily lives without our even knowing it.

Jon Stryker is heir to the Stryker Corporation, a medical device and technology company that brings in nearly $15 billion annually. In 2000, he founded the Arcus Foundation, which provides millions of dollars in grants to "LGBT" causes and to great ape sanctuaries. In 2015, it announced its plan to earmark $20 million specifically for "transgender" causes, and in 2021, Stryker donated $15 million to the ACLU to advance its "LGBT" causes in law and policy.[124] As a practical matter, because legal rights for

123 *Transsexual Empire*, 1994 Introduction, xxxv.
124 Dominic Holden, "Unprecedented $20 Million Announced for Transgender Causes," *Buzzfeed News* (December 8,

lesbians and gay men have largely been secured, this means advancing the ACLU's "gender identity" agenda in the courts and in state legislatures across the U.S., as described in Chapter 2.

Martine Rothblatt is a man who New York Magazine once described as "the highest paid female executive in America" in 2014.[125] Rothblatt once spent millions of dollars to create a robotic replica of his wife, Bina, and spoke about it publicly on NBC News in a piece called "Women who inspire: LGBTQ execs leading in technology."[126] Rothblatt is a multi-millionaire who pushes the "gender identity" agenda, in part, by publishing books with titles such as:

- Your Life or Mine: How Geoethics Can Resolve the Conflict Between Public and Private Interests in Xenotransplantation

- Unzipped Genes (America in Transition)

- The Apartheid of Sex: A Manifesto on the Freedom of Gender

- From Transgender to Transhuman: A Manifesto on the Freedom of Gender

Each of these titles is available on Amazon, and information about all of them is widely available. All of the language used is grounded in both the science and the politics of obliterating sex. The agenda is explicit.

At least one thing is for certain: rainbows sell products. During Pride Month (June) 2021, everyone who does not live under a rock was pummeled with images of rainbows and unicorns,

2015). ACLU, "ACLU Announces Jon L. Stryker and Slobodan Randjelovic LGBTQ & HIV Project" (March 4, 2021).
125   Lisa Miller, "The Trans-Everything CEO," *New York Magazine* (September 7, 2021).
126   Caroline Kim, "Women who inspire: LGBTQ execs leading in technology," NBC News (June 15, 2021).

all in the interest of selling more products and making more money. This has been going on for several years and has intensified of late. For example, there are Rainbow Doritos, Rainbow Vodka, and "gender-inclusive" umbrellas for sale.[127]

None of this corporate branding is done in the interest of advancing the very important cause of human rights for gay, lesbian, and bisexual people. Its purpose is to profit off of society's burgeoning insistence on hammering home to all of us the ludicrous idea that there is some category of people for whom sex is irrelevant. This is particularly tragic for the gay rights movement—a movement committed to the principle that same-sex attracted people are worthy of the same respect and freedom to associate as opposite-sex attracted people. If there is no such thing as sex, how can the law protect same-sex attraction?[128]

The point here is that "trans" is big business. Most of us have been taught that the fight for so-called "transgender rights" is a bottom-up grassroots movement to protect a vulnerable sexual minority. It is not. It is a top-down, corporate-driven enterprise designed to sell products and to maximize profits, being fueled by a small handful of extremely wealthy men whose very objective is to make us all forget that biological sex, not "gender identity," is grounded in material reality.

Of course, all this is happening in the context of a society that continuously, viciously, and brutally exploits female bodies.

One day, when I was twenty years old, I was standing on a street corner. I was in college, walking home from class, and standing at an intersection waiting for the light to turn. While I was standing there, a truck went through the intersection, and a man leaned out the window and yelled, "Hey, give me some of that pussy!" right at me. The truck drove away. Needless to say, the man faced no consequences for his actions. And that is not even

---

127   Peoplestaff225, "Alert, Alert, You Can Now Buy Rainbow-Colored Doritos," *People Magazine* (December 3, 2020). Absolute, "Absolute Rainbow," https://www.absolut.com/us/products/absolut-rainbow/. Target, "Pride Gender Inclusive Adult Rainbow Stick Umbrella," https://www.target.com/p/pride-gender-inclusive-adult-rainbow-stick-umbrella/-/A-81624193.

128   Lesbian and Gay News, "Obituary: The Rainbow Flag, previously a symbol of hope of the lesbian and gay civil rights movement, died in 2020 at the age of 42, writes Professional Judy," Lesbian and Gay News (April 29, 2021).

close to the worst example of how men have harassed, abused, and tortured me throughout my life. I am aware that many men will read this and think that I am making a big deal out of nothing. I have had men tell me as much. Plenty of women will think this too. There is a perfectly good reason for that—the systematic exploitation and abuse of women and girls has become so normal that it is virtually invisible, even as it stares us directly in the face.

But what does "gender identity" have to do with the sexual objectification of women? The answer is that it's complicated but worth exploring.

Sexual objectification "occurs when a woman's body or body parts are singled out and separated from her as a person and she is viewed primarily as a physical object of male sexual desire."[129] It is difficult to conceive of an example of singling out a woman's body parts and treating her as a physical object of male sexual desire than an anonymous man yelling at a young woman to "give me some of that pussy" and then driving away, never to be seen or heard from again. But sexual objectification of women does not happen only on an interpersonal level—it happens at the institutional and systemic levels as well.

Tarana Burke initially started using the phrase "me too" in her work supporting black girls who had survived sexual violence in 2006.[130] It caught on in the media after sexual assault accusations against Harvey Weinstein were made public in October 2017. That the "MeToo" movement got so much attention took me by surprise because I had assumed (naively, I suppose) that the rampant sexual abuse of women by men is obvious. I was taken aback that people seemed to be so surprised by the magnitude of the problem.

Some argue that sexual objectification of women doesn't exist—this is objectively untrue. The problem is not that it doesn't exist; the problem is that it is so prevalent that it becomes invisible. I once did an interview and told the story about the man who

---

129   Dawn M. Szymanski, Lauren B. Moffitt, and Erika R. Carr, "Sexual Objectification of Women: Advances to Theory and Research," American Psychological Association, 39 The Counseling Psychologist 1, 8 (2011).

130   Tarana Burke, "me too," https://metoomvmt.org/.

yelled at me to "give him some pussy." The man who was inter-
viewing me told me that it was my responsibility to decide how
to "interpret" the man's words. But I have to wonder, how many
ways are there to "interpret" this demand? The possibility of persuading men simply to stop behaving in this way is unthinkable
to most of us.

Our society is flooded with quasi-pornographic images of
half-naked women in bikinis and tight tank tops. I once complained to a male friend about having to be subjected to images
like these and his response was, "Well, some people like sex." That
totally misses the point. *Of course* some people like sex (most people, probably). But sexual objectification of women is not about
having a healthy sexuality. Most women look nothing like the
women pictured in these slickly produced commercial images, as
we all know, and many normal, average adult women manage to
have healthy sex lives, whether with men, women, or both.

Sexual objectification of women is not about sex—it is about
treating women like mere bodies to be used for male gratification.
This kind of objectification lies at the heart of "gender identity"
as well. This is true whether we are talking about men who claim
to be women, women who claim to be men, or anyone who claims
to be "non-binary."

In the case of men who pretend to be women, we are primarily talking about men who have a condition called "autogynephilia"—a sexual arousal at the thought of themselves as women—although some percentage of men pretending to be women are gay
men who are attracted to other men and are more comfortable
adopting a stereotypically "female" appearance. The term "autogynephilia" was coined in 1989 by Professor Ray Blanchard, who
derived it from Greek roots meaning "love of oneself as a woman"
and defined it as a male's propensity to be erotically aroused by
the thought or image of himself as female.[131] In doing so, he relied

---

131   Ray Blanchard, "Early History of the of the Concept of Autogynephilia," 34 Archives of Sexual Behavior 4, 439-
       446, 439 (September 2005).

primarily on the statements of men themselves—men who at the time were generally referred to as "transsexuals" in the same way that Janice Raymond used the term. The men in Blanchard's study made statements such as these:

> "An early experience I can still vividly remember of becoming aroused at the thought of becoming female was when I was approximately 9 or 10 years old. I was overweight and I had begun to develop breasts, solely from my weight. I would soap my breasts in the shower and imagine I was really a woman with a real woman's breasts, and I would become extremely aroused…

> …It wasn't until I actually started therapy that I began appearing in public dressed as a female. In the early days I would become aroused whenever anyone, a sales clerk, a casual stranger, would address me as "Ma'am" or perform some courtesy such as holding a door for me. This arousal led to a heightened fear of discovery, i.e., that my erection would give me away.

> I was imagining myself telling my parents, and my doctor, that I was really a girl. I imagined, in fact, lying down on the operating room table for my sex reassignment surgery. I was also imagining with horror that I would become sexually aroused. How would I explain this? How could I even understand for myself?

Wearing women's clothing and feminizing my body has always been sexually exciting for me—even after SRS [sex reassignment surgery]. ...it was and still is sexually exciting for me to have female body "functions." Before my SRS, I would pretend to menstruate by urinating in sanitary pads. I particularly enjoyed wearing the old fashion belted pad with long tabs.

My first experiences reading Playboy found me almost instantly aroused by the idea of being the model. When I was about 18, some friends took me to an old fashioned strip show, and I got aroused, all right—as soon as I got home, I put Noxzema cream on my nipples to simulate pasties! Even the idea of owning a girl's bike has aroused me."[132]

For these men, in other words, being sex objects lies at the heart of what it means to be female.

This point is made even more explicitly in the writings of some contemporary authors, such as Andrea Long Chu, a man who pretends to be a woman. In 2020, Chu published *Females*, a short book billed by its publisher as "An exploration of gender and desire from our most exciting new public intellectual," in which he stated, "pornography is what it feels like when you think you have an object, but really the object has you. It is therefore a quintessential expression of femaleness. Getting fucked makes you female because fucked is what a female is."[133] Chu also thinks that the essence of femaleness is being a vessel for another's desire.[134]

132   Blanchard, 440.
133   Andrea Long Chu, Females (Verso 2019).
134   Callie Hitchcock, "We are all female now," The *New Republic* (November 7, 2019).

The relationship between "transgender" and pornography is too complicated to explore in detail here, but I would be remiss if I did not at least mention today's booming porn industry, which depicts women's bodies in horrifically violent ways. The leading contemporary expert on how porn harms women and girls is Gail Dines, who has authored two important works on the topic: *Pornland: How Porn Has Hijacked Our Sexuality* and *Pornography: The Production and Consumption of Inequality*. I would encourage anyone interested in the influence of pornography on society's exploitation of women to read them and to consult her organization, Culture Reframed: Building Resilience & Resistance to Hypersexualized Media & Porn.[135]

One author who has done some of the best work researching the relationships between pornography and "transgender" is Genevieve Gluck, who addresses them in detail in her piece, "Why isn't anyone talking about the influence of porn on the trans trend?"[136] She discusses this in more detail in "Sissy Porn at Princeton University: Part 1 of a series on pornography and gender identity ideology."[137] Warning: this material is not for the faint of heart.

Gluck describes a 2020 presentation at Princeton University called "Forced Womanhood!" by a man named Rio Sofia. Sofia was presenting the contents of a 2017 exhibition at Cooper Union College, where Sofia displayed photographs and video of himself in sissification pornography (sissy pornography, or "forced femme"), where men are either "forced" or hypnotized into positions of sexual submission. They are allegedly made to wear makeup, dresses, and lingerie. The purpose of all of this is for the men who participate to become aroused at the thought of themselves being humiliated and degraded as though they were women.

This is Sofia's description of the 2017 exhibition:

---

135   Culture Reframed, https://www.culturereframed.org/.
136   Genevieve Gluck, who addresses it in her piece, "Why isn't anyone talking about the influence of porn on the trans trend?" Feminist Current (November 29, 2020).
137   Genevieve Gluck, "Sissy Porn at Princeton University: Part 1 of a series on pornography and gender identity ideology," Women's Voices (Substack) (May 30, 2021).

"Rio Sofia first encountered forced feminization pornography in 2015 while thumbing through fetish magazines at a shop in Manhattan. In sissification porn, where men are forced into womanhood as a form of punishment or humiliation, she found a rich underground [of] visual language that complicated her understanding of transgender representation. Within the context of BDSM, these depictions of gender transformation suggest coercion and a loss of (male) power, depictions that contradict developing narratives in the mainstream that celebrate gender transition as an empowering form of self-determination."

What he is saying here is that *"forced feminization" is erotic.* That being a woman is itself a form of punishment or humiliation. Male power is simply assumed. For him, to be a woman is itself to exist in a state of degradation and humiliation. To eroticize that displays an astonishing degree of misogyny.

Feminists are often criticized for exaggerating the extent to which we are objectified, exploited, and reviled throughout society, and we are told that we hate men. Most of us do not hate men at all. In fact, feminists tend to have much more faith in the humanity of men than others do. Andrea Dworkin was pointing to this when she said, "I don't believe rape is inevitable or natural. If I did, I would have no reason to be here. If I did, my political practice would be different than it is. Have you ever wondered why we [women] are not just in armed combat against you? It's not because there's a shortage of kitchen knives in this country. It is because we believe in your humanity, against all the evidence."[138]

---

138   Andrea Dworkin, "I want a 24-Hour Truce During Which There is No Rape" (1983), in Letters From a War Zone), 169-170.

The truth is that the pitiful ways in which women are treated are all right out there in the open. They are evident in the ways in which men catcall us, the ways in which we are depicted in imagery throughout society, the ways in which we are sexually harassed and abused, the ways in which we are objectified, and in pornography. "Gender identity" does not erase any of it. In fact, "gender identity" makes the objectification of women much, much worse because objectification of women is the essence of what "gender identity" is.

None of this is an accident. It's essentially a software upgrade to improve the system in which men control all the levers of power. U.K. feminist Jo Brew explains this well when she says:

> "The reason transgenderism has spread like wildfire through professions and organizations worldwide is that it is a new operating system helping them do their job—implementing patriarchy. It feels right, it solves problems, it fixes glitches. In the old operating system, the growing acceptance of equality between men and women had led to calls for women to hold half of the top jobs, get paid half of the money, control half of the decision-making power. This tide was held back by the 'it takes a long time to change' argument for a few decades, but as more and more outsider women have joined the professions, the professions were being turned against patriarchy itself. The pillars of the patriarchy were crumbling.
>
> The new operating system (OS): we could call it *TG7.2* as if it were a new software upgrade for a smartphone, is a neat simple fix that works in many ways. Basically, the new OS functions so that whenever someone says 'woman,' if it suits you, you can simply insert a man who says he's

a woman instead. What is more, in *TG7.2*, there is no fixed definition of woman, so it can mean anything the man says it means at any given moment. This changing definition of 'woman' will be validated by the new OS, using techniques such as doublethink in which sex=gender and sex≠gender. The professionals in organizations should support this as far as they can, but where necessary allow old operating systems to run in parallel."[139]

The speakers at the Women's Liberation Front's February 2020 event were making precisely this argument when we titled it "Fighting the New Misogyny: A Feminist Critique of Gender Identity." During that event, I stated:

> "To be clear, I do not think that any of us actually want to be talking about gender identity at all. In addition to her feminist work, Lierre has spent her entire adult life and career fighting for the planet and its inhabitants. I suspect that Meghan would probably rather speak out against the violence of pornography and prostitution, and that Saba would prefer to spend her time ending the violence of racism. I would very much like to be fighting for reproductive sovereignty for women, including abortion on demand and without apology. All of us have spent our lives fighting for justice, in one way or another. And yet now we all find ourselves in the following situation: We have to talk about the violence, misogyny, and homophobia of gender identity because we have no choice but to do so. But, then, men forcing women to do things that we do not want to do is hardly novel."

---

139   Jo Brew, "Transgenderism: A New Operating System for Patriarchy," 4W (January 14, 2021).

In this passage, I was referring to Lierre Keith, Meghan Murphy, and Saba Malik, each of whom had spoken before me. I stand by those words today.

Sexual objectification of women is not new, and feminists have been fighting it for centuries. What *is* relatively new is the evolution of the view that women exist solely for sexual and reproductive purposes into the notion that "woman" isn't a meaningful category of human beings at all, but rather a concept—a figment of a man's imagination. If anyone can be a woman, then no one is a woman, and if a man can claim to exist as a woman by simply announcing that he is one, that is a complete mockery of womanhood. The very concept of the "transgender woman" is the ultimate expression of the denial of women's humanity.

In 1979, Raymond concluded her critical work *The Transsexual Empire* as follows:

> "It is a critical time for woman-identified women. Medicalized transsexualism represents only one more aspect of patriarchal hegemony. The best response women can make to this is to see clearly just what is at stake for us with respect to transsexualism and to assert our own power of naming who we are."[140]

This statement is as true today as it was then, although feminists would likely use "transgenderism" rather than "transsexualism" now. The trans agenda (regardless of whether we use "transgender" or "transsexual") has continued apace. The simple truth is that women are female and men are male. The "gender identity" industry is working hard to obscure that truth in furtherance of its goal of abolishing sex.

Don't let them get away with it.

---

140   *Transsexual Empire*, 177.

The Global Campaign to Protect Women's Sex-Based Rights

THE WOMEN'S HUMAN RIGHTS CAMPAIGN is a global organization, consisting almost solely of volunteers, which is fighting to maintain women's sex-based rights in the law all over the world. Its primary mechanism for advancing its agenda is the Declaration on Women's Sex-Based Rights (the Declaration).[141] I became actively involved in WHRC's work in 2020 and currently serve as Chair of the Committee on Law and Legislation at the international level and as President of the Board of Directors at the national level.

It is my hope that readers of this book will embrace the seriousness of this issue and join the global campaign to protect our hard-fought rights as women in the face of this pernicious assault—pernicious because it poses as a movement of liberation and, indeed, as an extension of the movement to liberate women.

The Declaration itself is too long to include here, but it can be summarized by saying that it reaffirms the sex-based rights of women and girls:

---

141   Women's Human Rights Campaign, "Declaration on Women's Sex-Based Rights," https://www.womensdeclaration.com/en/.

- We reaffirm motherhood as an exclusively female status.

- We reaffirm women's and girls' rights to physical and reproductive integrity and oppose their exploitation through surrogacy and related practices.

- We reaffirm women's rights to freedom of opinion and expression, peaceful assembly and association, and political participation.

- We reaffirm women's rights to fair play in sports.

- We reaffirm the need to end violence against women and girls, and to protect rights of children.[142]

We oppose all forms of discrimination against women and girls that result from replacing "sex" with "gender identity" in law, policy, and social practice. At the time of writing, the Declaration had been signed by over 20,000 individuals from 140 countries and by 379 distinct organizations.

At the international level, WHRC frequently responds to consultations from national and international bodies, including the United Nations, on issues involving women's sex-based rights, including women's health, violence against women, hate crimes, toilet provision, and sexual orientation. In March of 2021, WHRC gave a virtual presentation on women's sex-based rights at the NGO Committee on the Status of Women in New York. WHRC has distinct and active chapters all over the world, in six continents, fighting the enshrinement of "gender identity" in their own laws and policies.

---

142   Women's Human Rights Campaign, "The shortest summary," https://www.womensdeclaration.com/en/declaration-womens-sex-based-rights-summary/.

The U.S. chapter of WHRC, which launched in 2020, is actively involved in efforts to advance the Declaration and stop the spread of "gender identity" in the U.S. at the federal and state levels. WHRC USA representatives have met with staff members from key House and Senate offices and submitted volumes' worth of testimony before state legislatures (primarily to protect women's sports).

In an effort to stop the Equality Act, WHRC USA sent a letter to Senate Majority Leader Charles Schumer, signed by thousands of women all over the world, stating:

> "Although the enactment of the Equality Act would only affect U.S. women directly, we are terrified of the impact that such enactment is likely to have globally. Our governments look to your government for leadership, expertise, and guidance. Already, we are seeing the word sex being redefined to include "gender identity" in laws throughout the U.K., the European Union, Australia, Canada, and New Zealand. These laws have had devastating impacts on the lives of women and girls, including the rapes of vulnerable women in prison, the inclusion of men in women's spaces such as locker rooms and changing rooms, and the inclusion of men in women's sports. This situation will only get worse if this law passes in the U.S., and similar laws are likely to extend to other geographic areas as well."[143]

As of this writing, Majority Leader Schumer has taken no known further action to advance the Equality Act on the floor of the Senate.

On March 16, 2021, WHRC USA submitted written testimony to the U.S Senate Judiciary Committee, which was sched-

---

143   Women's Human Rights Campaign U.S. chapter, "Our Letter to Senate Majority Leader Schumer" (March 6, 2021), https://womensdeclarationusa.com/our-letter-to-senate-majority-leader-charles-schumer/.

uled to hold a hearing on the bill the following day (I was the primary author of the testimony). In that testimony, we offered three main arguments:

- The nation simply has not had the national conversation that we need to have about the far-reaching implications of redefining sex to include so-called "gender identity," which the current version of the bill would do. We need to have that conversation before any legislation is enacted that would redefine sex to include so-called "gender identity."

- Simply put, men aren't women, even if they say they are, and even if they claim to "identify" as such. Women and girls need separate spaces from male people, also known as men and boys. There is no credible scientific evidence to support the proposition that a person born with a Y chromosome can be a woman. It is appalling that these things need to be said in the 21st century.

- Children are being permanently harmed at the altar of so-called "gender identity," whether the Democrats on the Committee are willing to recognize it or not.[144]

The Committee passed the bill over our objections.

At the executive level, WHRC USA has submitted numerous letters to the Biden administration expressing our disgust with the administration's strategy of abolishing sex and offered live testimony before the Department of Education regarding the importance of maintaining the category of sex for Title IX purposes.[145]

---

144   Women's Human Rights Campaign U.S. chapter, "WHRC Senate Judiciary Committee Testimony" (March 16, 2021), https://womensdeclarationusa.com/whrc-senate-judiciary-committee-testimony/.
145   Women's Human Rights Campaign U.S. chapter, "WHRC USA Gives Title IX Live Testimony" (June 8, 2021), https://womensdeclarationusa.com/whrc-usa-gives-title-ix-live-testimony/.

At the federal judicial level, WHRC USA submitted an *amicus* brief in the case of *Hecox v. Little*, described above.[146] In its brief, WHRC USA quoted the Declaration extensively, including (and especially) Article 7:

> "The Declaration is firm on this point: "To ensure fairness and safety for women and girls, the entry of boys and men who claim to have female 'gender identities' into teams, competitions, facilities, or changing rooms, inter alia, set aside for women and girls should be prohibited as a form of sex discrimination."

As noted earlier, that case has been sent from the appellate court back to the lower court to examine some factual questions and make a determination as to whether the case is moot.

WHRC USA rarely weighs in at the local level but made an exception when, on June 21, 2021, it teamed up with the Women's Liberation Front to send a letter to the Loudoun County, Virginia, school board, asking it not to proceed with its plan to obliterate single-sex spaces throughout the school district.[147] The letter was sent to every member of the board individually. The board was scheduled to vote on June 22nd, but instead, it decided to postpone the decision until August. On August 12, 2021, the board voted to approve the proposal over our objections.

We all need to be asking ourselves: What kind of world do we want to live in, and what steps are we willing to take to realize it? We can live in a world where public policy is grounded in material reality and the rights, privacy, and safety of women are protected—but we are going to have to fight for it. We can win, but even if we don't, only if we fight can we truthfully say that our government officials were warned about what was coming. This is

---

146   Women's Human Rights Campaign U.S. chapter, "*Amicus* brief filed, *Hecox v. Little*" (November 19, 2020), https://womensdeclarationusa.com/?s=Hecox.

147   Women's Human Rights Campaign U.S. chapter, "WHRC USA and WoLF Issue Joint Statement to Loudoun County Virginia School Board" (June 21, 2021), https://womensdeclarationusa.com/?s=Loudon.

true for everyone across the political spectrum. People reach out to me all the time via email and social media wanting to know what they can do. Countless Democrats are furious with our party leadership about its insistence on enshrining "gender identity" in law and policy. Republicans understand that it is Democrats who are driving this but are also frustrated with their own party leadership's seeming failure to stop it.

On September 29, 2021, a delegation of WHRC USA met with the staff of a senator in New York state to oppose the redefinition of sex to include "gender identity and expression" in the state constitution. The delegation consisted of two New York residents and me, all of us signatories to the Declaration on Women's Sex-Based Rights.

WHRC USA Vice President Lauren Levey, who lives in New York, initially reached out to request the meeting. The senator was receptive and scheduled the meeting promptly. We met with two young staff members, one woman and one man. Our aim was to explain why the redefinition of sex to include "gender identity and expression" harms everyone, women and girls in particular, and to request a statewide conversation about the impact that the new definition would have on women and girls. The other member of our delegation was Julie DeLisle, also a New York resident and the New York state contact for WHRC. The senator whose staff we met with was a Democrat in a mixed-party jurisdiction. She was elected in 2020, barely inching out a win over the Republican candidate, who won approximately 49 percent of the vote.

The bill we were discussing was a set of 2019 proposed amendments to the state constitution. The existing constitution provided for equal protection on the bases of race, color, creed, or religion. The amendments would add "ethnicity, national origin, age, disability, or sex including pregnancy, sexual orientation, gender identity or expression" to the list of protected categories. The senate had passed these amendments in 2019, but the bill had stalled since then. We were concerned only with the phrase "gender identity or expression," not with the inclusion of any of the other categories.

After explaining our concerns, which have been described in detail throughout this book, we offered an additional perspective that the senator, and other Democrats, might want to take into consideration. Although WHRC USA is non-partisan, all three members of our delegation were life-long Democrats. We know that there are countless rank and file Democrats across the country who are furious with Democratic party leadership because of what the party is doing on the topic of "gender identity." I told the staffers that I personally know one woman in New York who changed her party affiliation from Democrat to Independent because of this issue. I know several others outside the state who have done the same. I know one woman in Colorado, a life-long Democrat, who changed her party affiliation from Democrat to Republican because of this issue and immediately became active in her local Republican women's group. I even know two women, both active Democrats, who did the unthinkable in November 2020 and voted for Donald Trump *because of this issue.*

I told them that Democrats are angry because redefining the word sex to include "gender identity" is anti-woman, anti-gay, and anti-lesbian. I also told them that women are leaving the U.K. Labour Party in droves for the same reason. They are disgusted by Labour's embrace of "gender identity" ideology, which is sexist, homophobic, and anti-science. I told them that the Democrat party leadership ignores us at their peril. I asked them to help spread our message.

What can you do if you are politically conservative? Talk with fellow conservatives. Tell them to stop using the language of the opposition. If you mean men and boys, say men and boys. Use the language of biological reality. Talk with Republican party leadership and tell them the same thing. Although it is Democrats who are pushing "gender identity," the Republican party is not doing anyone any favors by continuing to use wrong-sex pronouns or vague language. I frequently talk with rank-and-file Republicans who are fed up with their party leadership's seeming ineptitude in fighting back. You can help guide them.

What can you do if you are politically liberal? Talk with fellow liberals. Ask them what they really think about this. Ask them if they know what is going on. If they fight for so-called "trans rights," ask them if they know what that really means. Ask them if they know that "gender identity" is a politically regressive movement that fortifies misogynistic and homophobic stereotypes. They probably don't. You can help educate them using the information contained here. Talk with your elected officials. If they are Democrats, tell them that numerous liberals are leaving the party because they are disgusted by party leadership's insistence on enshrining "gender identity" in the law.

Anyone can do this. You don't have to be a lawyer or any kind of professional. You just have to be a concerned citizen. Whoever you are and whatever your political inclinations, get online and find out what your state is doing on the topic of "gender identity." Schedule a meeting. Pick up the phone. You may not persuade your public officials that "gender identity" is a war on the material reality of biological sex. You may not convince them that it harms women and girls. But you will have told them, and then they can never say that they didn't know.

WHRC USA sees clearly that all of these efforts to abolish sex throughout law and society are having a devastating impact on women and girls, and we will not stop fighting them. We will never give up, and we hope that you will join us. If you want to get involved in the fight against the abolition of sex, please sign the Declaration on Women's Sex-Based Rights. All of humanity depends on it.

Acknowledgements

THIS BOOK WOULD NOT HAVE BEEN POSSIBLE without a few extremely important people to whom I express my eternal gratitude.

First is a dear friend and sister, who, in 2014, shot an arrow of awareness through me when she woke me up to the harm of "transgender." I was in the process of ending a ten-year abusive relationship, and her support was critical to my survival. One day, we were talking all things political, and feminist, and I mentioned the rights of "transgender" people. She stopped me in my tracks and said, "No. All of transgenderism is misogynistic and antithetical to radical feminism." I asked her to elaborate, and she did, and she concluded by saying, "Think about it, Kara, it's the ultimate penetration of our bodies by men." My life has not been the same since, and I am forever in her debt for waking me up. Understandably, for her privacy and safety, and for other reasons explained in this volume, she has asked me not to use her name. She knows who she is.

Second is Lierre Keith, who did the entire world a huge favor by founding the Women's Liberation Front (WoLF) in 2013. WoLF is, in my view, one of the most important organizations fighting for the rights, privacy, and safety of women and girls in the U.S. today, and I had the honor of serving on its board from 2016 to 2020. Lierre works tirelessly to save the earth and its inhabitants, and she will never cave in her determination to protect women and girls on the basis of sex. Our friendship has survived some difficult times, and I will always consider her a friend and mentor.

Third is Sheila Jeffreys, a hero to women and girls all over the world and a co-author of the Declaration on Women's Sex-Based Rights. Her work in pointing out that "gender identity" is a movement for men's sexual entitlement has been critical in advancing the fight to protect women and girls on the basis of sex.

Fourth is Amy Dansky, my grandmother, who taught me what it means to be a fierce warrior woman in a world dominated by men and to think critically, always. She died in 2007. When Justice Ruth Bader Ginsburg died, I expressed the thought: "If there is any silver lining, may it be that she is with my Jewish grandmother, wherever Jewish grandmothers go when they die." My father's response was that "Jewish grandmothers do not die; they live on in the hearts of their granddaughters." Here's to you, Grandma Amy.

Finally is my partner, Jeff. When we started dating, he wondered how I could hold such left-leaning views on most things and also hold the views about the abolition of sex that I have expressed here. But he listened to me and, along the way, came to understand the dire consequences for all of society of the abolition of sex. He is living proof that we can all see through the madness once we open our eyes.

About the Author

Author Photo by Tina Glass

KARA DANSKY IS A FEMINIST, attorney, and public speaker. She serves as the Chair of the Committee on Law and Legislation for the global Women's Human Rights

Campaign (WHRC) and President of the WHRC's U.S. chapter. She served on the board of the Women's Liberation Front from 2016-2020 and remains a member of that organization. She has a twenty-year background in criminal law and criminal justice policy, having worked at the Mayor's Office of Criminal Justice in New York, the American Civil Liberties Union, the Stanford Criminal Justice Center at Stanford Law School, and the Society of Counsel Representing Accused Persons in Seattle. She also clerked at the U.S. District Court for the District of New Mexico and was a staff attorney at the U.S. Court of Appeals for the Third Circuit.

Made in the USA
Coppell, TX
08 January 2022